**Editors**
Gillian Eve Makepeace, M.S.
Sara Connolly

**Illustrator**
Clint McKnight

**Cover Artist**
Brenda DiAntonis

**Editor In Chief**
Ina Massler Levin, M.A.

**Creative Director**
Karen J. Goldfluss, M.S. Ed.

**Art Production Manager**
Kevin Barnes

**Art Coordinator**
Renée Christine Yates

**Imaging**
Nathan P. Rivera
Ariyanna Simien

*Publisher*

*Mary D. Smith, M.S. Ed.*

Includes Standards

# MEDIA LITERACY

Grade **6**

- Acquire tools to become media literate
- Learn about a variety of forms of media
- Interpret the true messages in media

**Author**

## Melissa Hart, M.F.A.

**Teacher Created Resources, Inc.**
12621 Western Avenue
Garden Grove, CA 92841
www.teachercreated.com

ISBN: 978-1-4206-2779-

©2008 Teacher Created Resourc
Reprinted, 2017
Made in U.S.A.

D1089678

Teacher Created Resources

# Table of Contents

# Table of Contents *(cont.)*

# Foreword

At its core, this book teaches children and young people how to think critically about media messages, particularly visual media messages.

As the author points out, we are subjected to thousands of mediated images each day. They flash by us so fast that we have no time to think about them. Indeed most are designed to by-pass critical thought. They are carefully crafted to be felt. They tap into our emotions—fear, insecurity, sentimentality, prejudices. Often they purport to portray reality so that, with time, we unquestioningly treat them as being true, and we shape our behavior accordingly, divorced from the world around us.

Nowhere in our formal education have we been taught how to assess and critique these messages and so we have been buffeted by their impact, whether in the purchase of unneeded products, in how we perceive our abilities, or in the way we vote on Election Day. Media education, on the other hand, helps students become smarter in all aspects of their lives.

This book, with its fascinating and fun exercises, is intended to prepare children, a new generation, to see—literally—media images differently, critically. Once given the tools to analyze and think about what they see, children are astonishingly perceptive.

Students are shown how to put their newly acquired skills and insights to use. The skills learned here (and as presented, they are fun to learn) will carry over into other disciplines. Critical thinking about media statistics connects with math. Realizing the role of media-caused anxiety tells us much about psychology and even politics. Analyzing how stories are compellingly told on the screen teaches about clear, vivid writing. The list goes on and on.

More than learning how to make thoughtful, informed decisions and to shape a new, questioning relationship with media, young people also learn how to transform their lives. They perceive themselves differently and more positively. They soon learn that media literacy skills can be applied to all aspects of life.

Young people are great teachers. The great hope is that they will share their new knowledge with their parents and other adults so that, as a society, we all will become more aware and media literate.

Over the years, the media, which have such great potential to perform good, have done greater and greater harm. We have seen an exponential growth in irresponsible content—more violence, more commercialism, more sexualization, more fear-mongering, and more deception. Public service has become a rarity. The one sure way to reverse the trend is for audiences to become media literate— for them to recognize the personal and societal consequences of irresponsible media messages and media consumption.

If audiences find such messages unfit for consumption and reject them, media decision-makers must change the media. Indeed, a media-literate public, armed with the tools taught in this text and elsewhere, has the power to force media to redeem themselves and fulfill their great potential and promise.

*—Rick Seifert and Rebecca Woolington*
*MediaThink*

# How to Use this Book

Media surrounds us, from the moment we wake up in the morning until we go to bed at night. *Media Literacy, Grade 6* gives students the opportunity to study most forms of media to which they are exposed almost every day. Each assignment conforms to one or more of the McREL standards for grade six, as noted on pages six and seven.

The book begins with a general discussion of media literacy, of the various forms of media and how consumers are exposed to it. Students are asked to chart their own media consumption, and to examine several forms of media for healthy and unhealthy messages including propaganda and stereotypes.

Historical overviews of each genre in media preface each section of the book. These descriptions allow students to understand how a particular genre has changed over time, or has given way to a new form of media. Photographs from the National Archives and the Library of Congress offer students the opportunity to view and analyze examples of media from the past and compare them to contemporary media.

In each section of the book, students are asked to deconstruct media in a variety of ways, through multiple choice questions, matching exercises, compositions, reviews, and charts. Many assignments require research with the use of books, encyclopedias, and/or the Internet. Each section concludes by offering students the opportunity to create a tangible example of the media genre they have studied. These hands-on projects can be completed alone or in small groups. They offer numerous opportunities for group discussion, and for demonstration among students and for parents.

*Image Courtesy of the Library of Congress, Prints and Photographs Division (LC-USZC2-1086)*

A final project allows students to choose a favorite form of media and create an example. Later, they are asked to deconstruct what they have created to demonstrate a working knowledge of media literacy. A certificate on page 131 of the book can be reproduced and passed out to students as an acknowledgement of completing this book.

The final page offers you, the teacher, additional resources for the study of media literacy, including websites, organizations, and books. We hope that *Media Literacy, Grade 6* will become a valuable addition to your classroom and curriculum.

# Standards

## Introduction

Each lesson in *Media Literacy, Grade 6*, meets one or more of the following standards, which are used with permission from McREL (Copyright 2007, McREL, Mid-continent Research for Education and Learning.  Telephone: 303/337-0990.  Website:  **www.mcrel.org.**)

| Standard | Pages |
|---|---|
| Understands connections among the various art forms and other disciplines | all |
| Understands that group and cultural influences contribute to human development, identity, and behavior | 19-25, 51–52, 63, 70, 79–82, 92–94, 98, 101–102, 112–114, 122–124 |
| Understands what is meant by "the public agenda," how it is set, and how it is influenced by public opinion and the media | 18–25, 63, 66, 71, 90–95, 98–99, 101–102, 112–113, 117, 119, 122 |
| Knows environmental and external factors that affect individual and community health | 18–25, 55, 63, 79, 80, 82, 86, 92–95, 98, 101–102, 123, 124 |
| Understands the historical perspective | 39–41, 46, 51–52, 56, 70, 84, 87–88, 97, 105, 106, 112, 114–119, 122 |
| Uses the general skills and strategies of the writing process, and Uses the stylistic and rhetorical aspects of writing, Uses grammatical and mechanical conventions in written compositions | 13, 16, 20, 35, 34, 50, 55, 58–60, 62, 64, 68, 69, 75, 79, 81, 82, 84, 85, 99–102, 104, 110, 113, 119, 122 |
| Gathers and uses information for research purposes | 12, 13, 18, 20, 27–35, 34, 47–50, 51–53, 57, 58–60, 65–67, 73, 77–82, 90, 91, 94, 96, 99, 100, 103, 105, 111–113, 115, 119, 122–129 |
| Uses the general skills and strategies of the reading process to understand and interpret a variety of literary and informational texts | 10, 11, 13–16, 38, 46, 51–54, 56, 65, 70, 73, 76, 77, 83–85, 92, 97, 98, 99, 108–109, 112–114, 122 |
| Uses listening and speaking strategies for different purposes | 46–55, 72, 82, 130 |
| Uses viewing skills and strategies to understand and interpret visual media | 26–32, 58–66, 74–79, 86, 91–96, 98, 101–103, 106, 108–109, 112–117, 119–130 |
| Understands the characteristics and components of the media | all |

# Standards *(cont.)*

| Standard | Pages |
|---|---|
| Understands the relationship between music and history and culture | 71, 73 |
| Understands the relationships among science, technology, society, and the individual | 80–82, 89, 126–130 |
| Understands the nature and uses of different forms of technology | 46, 56, 75, 76, 126–130 |
| Understands and applies the basic principles of presenting an argument, Understands and applies basic principles of logic and reasoning | 71, 82, 85, 109 |
| Effectively uses mental processes that are based on identifying similarities and differences | 36, 43, 44, 61, 76, 87, 88, 95, 101, 102, 122–124 |
| Understands and applies media, techniques, and processes related to the visual arts | all |
| Knows a range of subject matter, symbols, and potential ideas in the visual arts | all |
| Understands the visual arts in relation to history and cultures | 27–32, 39, 97, 106, 114–117, 119, 122, 126 |
| Understands the characteristics and merits of one's own artwork and the artwork of others | 37, 45, 89, 104, 118, 120 |
| Contributes to the overall effort of a group | 45, 55, 62, 75, 82, 89, 104, 125, 130 |

# What Is Media Literacy?

Each morning, you wake up and get ready for the day. Maybe you listen to the radio or watch a little television. Maybe you glance at the newspaper, or flip through a magazine. You may even play a few minutes of a videogame or surf the Internet.

Outside, you may walk past billboards or ride a bus with ads above the seats. You may decide to see a movie or listen to a good band. You may study a piece of art, or shop for a favorite item.

Each day, you see and hear dozens of forms of media.

The word **media** refers to all the different ways in which people communicate. Each of the examples above represents a type of media.

The word **literacy** means education. Someone who is **media literate** understands how people create media, and how this media affects others.

By the end of this book, you will understand:
- why so many snacks come in red packages.
- why sometimes you can spot your favorite soda in a movie.
- why people in magazine ads are very attractive.
- why newspapers from three different countries tell the same story three different ways.
- how people who make commercials get you to buy their products.
- why you believe you need that new video game.
- what you don't even know you're seeing as you surf the Internet.

Prepare to be amazed as you enter the amazing world of media!

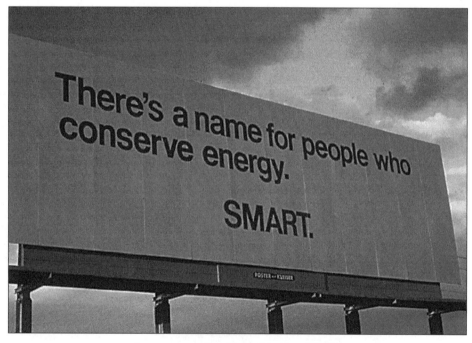

*Image courtesy of The National Archives (555380)*

# Forms of Media

Most people see and hear hundreds of forms of media every day. Media is all around us. It directly affects our view of the world. Some sources of media, and their effects, are well known. Here are some examples:

- A 12-year old girl sees an advertisement for perfume. In the ad, a beautiful woman floats smiling above the clouds. The girl believes that if she wears the scent, she will be pretty and happy. She buys the perfume.

- A young man hears the same song over and over on the radio. He buys the band's album. Then, he learns the song. He believes that if he knows a popular song, people will see him as popular, too.

- Two sixth-graders see a movie in which the main character uses one brand of computer to solve a crime. They ask their parents to buy this computer. They believe that it will allow them to solve a crime.

Other sources of media, and their effects, may surprise you! Here are some examples:

- A 12-year old goes to the local art museum. He studies a photo of a handsome, fit swimmer. He enrolls in swimming lessons. With them, he believes he will become handsome and fit, too.

- A young woman goes to her favorite homepage on the Internet and reads the news. Without thinking about it, she notes an ad for a brand of soda. When she logs off her computer, she goes to the store to buy a bottle of the soda.

Here are some of the most common forms of media:

- radio
- websites
- movies
- television
- newspapers
- mail
- billboards
- books
- magazines
- print ads
- photos
- speeches
- radio
- paintings
- e-mail
- sculptures
- videogames
- packages

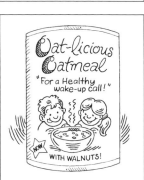

# How Much Media?

**Directions:** Complete the activities 1–3 below.

1. Study the list on the previous page. Then, write down all the forms of media you are exposed to each day.

   _____       _____
   _____       _____
   _____       _____
   _____       _____
   _____       _____

2. Now, make a chart that shows how many hours a day you see and hear each type of media, according to the example below.

| Type of Media | Hours Per Day Used |
|---|---|
| television | two hours |
|  |  |
|  |  |
|  |  |
|  |  |
|  |  |
|  |  |
|  |  |
|  |  |
|  |  |
|  |  |
|  |  |
|  |  |

3. Study your chart. In the space below, describe what you found out about the type and amount of media you consume. Explain anything that surprised you.

   _____
   _____
   _____
   _____

# Media's Importance to You

As you know now, media is all around you. It affects how you view yourself and your life. It shapes the choices you make. Media tells you to listen to a particular song, buy a certain brand of shoes, or choose a movie to watch.

Media creators know this. They understand that if they put a beautiful girl in a newspaper ad for a certain cell phone, many people will want to buy that phone. They know that when they put a song in a popular movie, many people will leave the theater wanting to buy that music.

Your favorite form of media makes you feel a certain way. It affects your life in a specific manner, as well. For instance, a girl who reads a popular book series may feel happy and smart. She may feel her heart racing as she turns the pages. She might find that she hurries through homework and walking the dog so she can have more time to read. She may even find that reading these books has inspired her to become a writer.

**Directions:** In the space below, write down your favorite form of media. Refer to the list you made on page 10. Then, explain how your favorite form of media makes you feel and how it affects your life.

_____

_____

_____

_____

_____

_____

_____

_____

_____

_____

_____

_____

_____

_____

_____

_____

_____

# Analyzing Media

Want to understand a butterfly's wing? Chances are you will look at it under a magnifying glass. You might even study it under a microscope.

Likewise, if you want to be a gymnast, you will break down your routine into small actions. You will perfect each action. Finally, you will see just how to do a back flip and a handstand.

*Analyzing* means breaking down a large object or action into smaller pieces.

Media literate people are able to analyze its many forms. Watch or listen to one type of media. Then, ask yourself the following questions:

- Who paid for this media? (Did a company pay? Did one person pay?)
- To what age group and gender does this media appeal? (Does it appeal to 12-year-old students, or to retired adults your grandmother's age?)
- What is the obvious message in this media? (You should buy this toboggan.)
- What are the hidden messages in this media? (If you buy this toboggan, you will have many friends.)
- In what ways is this a healthy and/or an unhealthy example of media? (The toboggan is healthy as it's an activity outside, but riding without a helmet or other protection is not.)

Advertisement from 1886 for Star Toboggans

*Image courtesy of the Library of Congress, Prints and Photographs Division (LC-USZ62-19184)*

# Methods of Advertising

People who make media know how to shape your desires. They use images and sounds carefully. Want to be media literate? Learn the following methods of advertising.

**Directions:** The next two pages list methods of advertising. Study the list and examples below.

| Method | Example |
|---|---|
| **Bandwagon**—this method says that everyone else is doing it, so why aren't you? | All the kids listen to this band. You should, too. |
| **Beautiful People**—good-looking models make us think we can look like them. | I'll look like him or her if I wear this shirt. |
| **Bribery**—this offers something we want in return for something we do or buy. | Buy this car, and we'll enter you in a contest! |
| **Fear**—sometimes, media makes us afraid. It tells us that if we don't buy something, something bad could happen. | Buy this bottled water, or you will get sick. |
| **Flattery**—if you compliment someone, he or she will pay attention. | You're so smart because you wear that brand of jeans. |
| **Humor**—making someone laugh is one method of advertising. | This magazine ad about kids who eat one brand of donut is funny. I want to buy that brand! |
| **Hyperbole**—this is another word for exaggeration. | Our fruit juice will give you super-powers! |
| **Name Calling**—characters make fun of other characters to sell something. | That child is strange because he does not own that action figure. |
| **Plain Folks**—people just like us use the same product. | That guy with the chewing gum looks like me, so I should buy this chewing gum. |
| **Repetition**—hearing or seeing something over and over gets a brand-name to stay in your head. | You should shop at Candy's Fashions because their clothes will make you look as sweet as candy. |
| **Scientific Evidence**—statistics and charts make us think that we should buy something. | Four out of five doctors recommend this vitamin for growing children. |
| **Symbols**—these are words, places, images, and songs that represent something else. | An olive branch is a symbol of peace. |
| **Testimonials**—famous people sell products and ideas. | These Olympic ice skaters wear this type of lip gloss, so I should, too! |
| **The Big Lie**—believe it or not, sometimes media makers do not tell the truth. | Your friends will envy you if you buy this videogame. |
| **Warm and Fuzzy**—cute, sweet images sell stuff. | That little puppy likes this brand of dog food. My dog will, too. |

# Advertising in Action

A *slogan* is a line used by the media. It advertises a product or action. You can study a slogan for methods of advertising. Here are some examples:

- You'll score at the box office in Movie Star Shoes.

  (Method of Advertising: Beautiful People—movie stars are usually attractive.)
- Don't lose your head—wear your bike helmet!

  (Method of Advertising: Fear—if you don't wear a bike helmet, you might get killed!)

**Directions:** Write down one slogan from the media, below. Then, list its method of advertising.

_____

_____

_____

_____

A **jingle** is a short song or poem. It is used by the media to advertise a product or action. A jingle has a method of advertising, just like a slogan. Here is an example:

> **"If you like clean air,**
>
> **safe for you and me,**
>
> **show the world you care—**
>
> **stop and plant a tree!"**

Here are the methods of advertising for this jingle:

- symbols—a tree is a symbol for clean air
- fear—if you don't plant a tree, our air will be dirty
- bandwagon—show everyone that you care
- bribery—if you plant a tree, we'll have clean air

**Directions:** Create a jingle and write it down below. List its methods of advertising.

_____

_____

_____

_____

_____

# Hidden Messages

You need to be able to see a piece of media and understand what messages it has. Such messages are both obvious and hidden. A television ad for a sports car might show a handsome man in the driver's seat. Three beautiful women might look at him and smile. The obvious message of this ad is that you should buy this car. The hidden message of this ad is that if you buy this car, you will be good-looking and happy. Attractive people will like you.

**Directions:** Read the descriptions of media below. Then, explain the obvious message and the hidden message.

1. In a television commercial, a girl drinks chocolate milk. Suddenly, she can dance like a rock star and is surrounded by good-looking people who love her.

| Obvious Message | Hidden Message |
|---|---|
|  |  |

2. On a radio show for children, the host talks to a scientist. "I did four hours of homework a night," says the scientist, "and now I'm a millionaire."

| Obvious Message | Hidden Message |
|---|---|
|  |  |

3. On a billboard, there is a photo of a bouquet of flowers on a smashed up bicycle. The text says, "Wear your helmet… for life."

| Obvious Message | Hidden Message |
|---|---|
|  |  |

# Propaganda

*Propaganda* is the use of false details to sell things or ideas. In 1889, newspaper owner William Randolph Hearst asked an artist to make propaganda. He wanted the artist to draw Cubans fighting Spanish people in the Spanish-American War.

The artist sent a message to Hearst. He said that he saw no signs of war.

Hearst said that he would make up details about war in his newspaper. "You provide the pictures," he replied, "and I'll provide the war."

Why did Hearst use propaganda? A war story sells newspapers!

**Directions:** Study the World War I poster on page 17. Then, read the questions below and choose the letter that best completes the sentence for each question. Write a sentence underneath explaining why you chose that answer.

1. The idea sold by this poster is that the Army offers

    **a.** a horse
    **b.** adventure
    **c.** wagons

    _____

    _____

    _____

2. The method of advertising used here is:

    **a.** fear
    **b.** warm and fuzzy
    **c.** bribery

    _____

    _____

    _____

3. The office that paid for this ad wants to get people to:

    **a.** enlist in the Army
    **b.** buy a horse
    **c.** go on a vacation

    _____

    _____

    _____

*Image courtesy of the Library of Congress, Prints and Photographs Division (LC-USZC4-7577)*

# Making Propaganda

*Propaganda* is the use of false information to sell a product or idea.

**Directions:** Study a newspaper or magazine advertisement. Find one that uses propaganda and draw a picture of the ad below. Then, answer the questions.

1. What product or idea is this advertisement attempting to sell?

   _____

2. What method of advertising is used here?

   _____

   _____

3. How does this media-maker use propaganda?

   _____

   _____

4. Now, create your own ad. Use propaganda. Choose an idea or product that you want to sell. Draw an ad on a piece of paper. Make sure it has a slogan. Include an image that helps to show propaganda.

# Stereotypes

A *stereotype* is general description of a person. It is often based on their looks. It is a simple, but untrue, way to describe someone. What do the words "dumb blond," "insensitive male," and "wicked stepmother" have in common? Each of these is an example of a stereotype.

Many forms of media use stereotypes. These simple words can hurt people. A blond girl might think that she is dumb. A boy might think that he is unkind. And a stepmother might worry that she is mean, all because of stereotypes.

**Directions:** Consider the following scenes. Each uses a stereotype. Describe who is being stereotyped and how. Then explain who this media might hurt. The first one has been done for you.

| Scenario | Who is Being Stereotyped and How? | Who Might be Hurt by this Media? |
|---|---|---|
| A car company films a new television commercial. In it, a Latino man tries to steal a car. An Anglo man in a business suit chases him down. He gets the car back and a beautiful woman joins him in the front seat. | The Latino man is being stereotyped as a car thief. The Anglo man is stereotyped as a success. | Latino people might be hurt by this image of them as dishonest. Anglo men might worry that they are not successful enough. |
| A newspaper runs an ad for a new grocery store. In it, a woman pushes a shopping cart through the aisle while a man sits in an easy chair in the deli. He is eating a sandwich. | | |
| A children's book shows a teddy bear with blond curls and a new dress. All the boy teddy bears want to be her friend. The girl bear with the red hair and old clothes does not have any friends. | | |

# Stereotypes *(cont.)*

**Directions:** Now write your own stereotypes. On the left-hand side of the chart, create a stereotype for a character and form of media. On the right side, create a true description free of stereotypes. The first one has been done for you.

| Character | Form of Media | Stereotype | Original |
|---|---|---|---|
| Doctor | Magazine ad | This magazine ad features an Anglo male. He is tall and handsome. He wears glasses and white coat. | This magazine ad features a black woman. She wears jeans and a white sweater. She is short, and of average weight. She has a wide smile. |
| Smart girl | Television commercial | | |
| Firefighter | Magazine ad | | |
| Babysitter | Movie | | |

# Healthy and Unhealthy Media

Healthy media sends good messages to people. It doesn't do anything to hurt their body or mind. An example of healthy media is a commercial at the movies that shows one child being nice to another.

Unhealthy media hurts people. A television program that shows boys being mean to the new kid at school because he does not own a brand-name skateboard is not healthy media. Kids who watch this show may begin to think that people will like them only if they own this brand-name skateboard.

**Directions:** Study the two forms of media on page 22. Circle true or false after the statements below about the media.

---

## Ad One

1. This poster from the 1940s is trying to get people to drink milk.

    True          False

2. This advertiser says that milk gives people cavities.

    True          False

3. The Milk Department paid for this poster.

    True          False

4. This poster says that if you drink milk, you will have strong bones.

    True          False

5. This is a healthy example of media.

    True          False

---

## Ad Two

1. This ad is trying to sell bees.

    True          False

2. Dr. Sugar is the name of a soda.

    True          False

3. In this ad, children love soda.

    True          False

4. The method of advertising in this ad is warm and fuzzy.

    True          False

5. This is an unhealthy form of advertising.

    True          False

**Ad One**

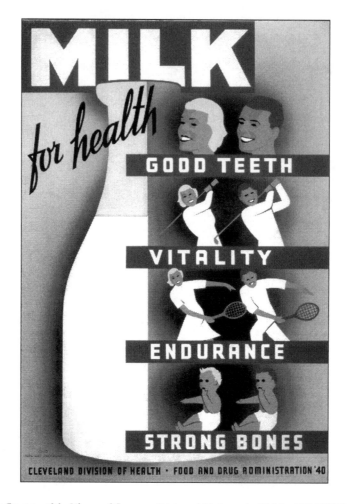

*Image Courtesy of the Library of Congress, Prints and Photographs Division (LC-USZC2-1086)*

**Ad Two**

Now it's your turn. In the spaces below, design one example of healthy media, and one example of unhealthy media. Then, write at least a paragraph about each, describing and explaining why you included certain things in each ad.

| Healthy Media | Unhealthy Media |
|---|---|
|  |  |

_____

_____

_____

_____

_____

_____

_____

_____

_____

# First Media

Prehistoric people made media called petroglyphs. These are drawing or carvings on rocks or in caves. They used petroglyphs to show what was around them. They made pictures about animals, weather, and people.

Here is a picture of a petroglyph near Montezuma Castle. It is found in Arizona. Native Americans made petroglyphs on this rock hundreds of years ago.

*Image courtesy of the Library of Congress, Prints and Photographs Division (LC-USZ62-113247)*

**Directions:** Study the photo of the petroglyphs. What do you think the pictures mean? Explain below.

_____

_____

_____

_____

_____

_____

_____

_____

_____

_____

_____

# Understanding Petroglyphs

**Directions:** Use encyclopedias, books, and the Internet to find a petroglyph you like. Copy the petroglyph into the space below. Then, write a sentence below each of the headings.

**Found at**

**Created by**

**Date created**

**Possible message**

# Make a Petroglyph

Develop symbols for words.  Then create a petroglyph of your own so you can send a message to people. You will need a small rock with one flat side, and paint and brushes.

**Directions:**

1. Fill out the symbol-chart below.  In the top row, write the words you will use on your petroglyph. On the bottom row, draw a symbol for each word.  An example has been done for you.

| Word | Love | | | | | | | |
|---|---|---|---|---|---|---|---|---|
| Symbol | ♥ | | | | | | | |

2. Now, make your petroglyph.  Use the paint and brushes to paint your symbols on your rock.

3. Finish your petroglyph.  Display it for others to see.  See if they can read your symbols correctly.

4. In the space below, write at least one paragraph to explain the message you wrote on your petroglyph.

26                        ©Teacher Created Resources, Inc.

# Print Ads

Print ads—on rock or paper—are a popular form of media. Most of us rely on our sight to give us clues about the world. Pictures and text are powerful.

On page 28 is an example of a print ad from 1861. You can deconstruct it like any other form of media.

**Directions:** Study the ad on page 28 and then answer the questions below. When you have finished, write a couple of sentences saying if you like or dislike the ad and why.

1. What product is being advertised?_____

2. Who paid for this ad?_____

3. To what age group and gender does this ad appeal? _____

4. What methods of advertising are used in this media? _____

5. What is the obvious message in this ad? _____

6. What are the hidden messages in this ad? _____

7. In what ways is this ad a healthy and/or unhealthy form of media? _____

---

## My Thoughts About This Ad

_____

_____

_____

_____

_____

_____

_____

_____

_____

_____

_____

_____

_____

_____

_____

_____

*Image courtesy of the Library of Congress, Prints and Photographs Division (LC-USZ62-4625)*

# Early Print Ads

**Directions:** Study the two ads on page 30—Ad One is from 1868 and Ad Two is from 1851. Complete the questions below for each ad.

1. What is being advertised?

   Ad One: _____

   Ad Two: _____

2. Who paid for these advertisements?

   Ad One: _____

   Ad Two: _____

3. To what age group and gender do these advertisements appeal?

   Ad One: _____

   Ad Two: _____

4. What advertising methods are used?

   Ad One: _____

   Ad Two: _____

5. What is the obvious message in these advertisements?

   Ad One: _____

   Ad Two: _____

6. What are the hidden message in these advertisements, if any?

   Ad One: _____

   _____

   Ad Two: _____

   _____

7. In what ways are these ads a healthy or unhealthy examples of media?

   Ad One: _____

   _____

   _____

   Ad Two: _____

   _____

   _____

**Ad One**

*Image courtesy of the Library of Congress, Prints and Photographs Division (LC-USZ62-2597)*

**Ad Two**

*Image courtesy of the Library of Congress, Prints and Photographs Division (LC-DIG-pga-00031)*

# Today's Print Ads

Advertising has changed a great deal over the years.  The next two pages ask you to study a print ad from today.

**Directions:**  Find a print ad in a magazine or newspaper.  Cut it out and paste it into the space below or draw the ad instead.

# Today's Print Ads *(cont.)*

**Directions:** Study the print advertisement from the previous page, then answer the questions below.

1. Who paid for this ad?

   _____

2. To what age group, economic group, and gender does this ad appeal?

   _____

3. What methods of advertising are used?

   _____

   _____

4. What is the obvious message in this ad?

   _____

   _____

   _____

5. What are the hidden messages in this ad?

   _____

   _____

   _____

6. In what ways is this ad a healthy and/or unhealthy example of media?

   _____

   _____

   _____

   _____

   _____

   _____

   _____

# Compare and Contrast

Print advertisement have changed a great deal over time. Images are different, as are language, messages, and techniques of persuasion. You can study how print ads have changed by comparing an early ad with another that has appeared recently in print.

**Directions:** Using books, encyclopedias, and the Internet, locate an early print advertisement. Possible search engine terms include *early print advertisement*, *historical advertisement*, and *pictorial Americana*. Sketch the ad you choose in the space below. Then, locate a contemporary print ad in a magazine or newspaper. Sketch this ad in the other space.

Finally, look at the questions below the boxes and using these to help you, complete the Venn diagram on page 34 comparing the two ads.

- How are these two ads similar or different in terms of text?
- How are these two ads similar or different in terms of images?
- What techniques of persuasion are similar or different in the two ads?
- How do you think print advertising has changed over the last 150 years? Give specific examples.

# Compare and Contrast *(cont.)*

**Directions:** Complete this Venn diagram to show how past and present ads differ. Also, explain how they are similar. In the circle on the left, write features of the ads from the past. In the circle on the right, write features of the ads from the present. Where the two circles overlap, put features that are common to both ads. In the space on the right, write a few sentences explaining how you think print advertising has changed over the last 150 years. Give specific examples.

**Ads from the Present**

**Ads from the Past**

# Make a Print Ad

Now it's your turn to show all that you have learned about print ads.

**Directions:** On a separate sheet of paper, make your own print ad for any product you would like, and then answer the questions below.

1. What product is being advertised?

   _____

2. What age group will like your ad?  Will it appeal to boys, girls, or both?

   _____

   _____

3. What methods of advertising do you use in your ad?

   _____

   _____

4. What are the obvious messages in your ad?

   _____

   _____

   _____

5. What are the hidden messages, if any?

   _____

   _____

   _____

6. How is your ad an example of healthy or unhealthy media?

   _____

   _____

   _____

   _____

   _____

# Billboards

Billboards are print advertisement on a grand scale. In 1835, a man named Jared Bell printed enormous posters—also called "bills"—to advertise a circus. He placed them outside, and introduced a new form of media! By 1867, advertisers leased space on the sides of buildings and on fences for their enormous ads. Now, you can see billboards every time you drive down a major street or highway.

*Image courtesy of the Library of Congress, Prints and Photographs Division (LC-USZ62-58982)*

How many products do you see advertised in this roadside photo from 1905?

---

*Image courtesy of the Library of Congress, Prints and Photographs Division (LC-USZ62-91461)*

Some billboards do not advertise particular products. Instead, they advertise actions or ideas. This billboard from Alabama celebrates those who live in the United States.

# Early Billboards

Some billboards are political. This billboard appeared in 1916, before all women in the United States had the right to vote.

**Directions:** Study the billboard below. Then, answer the questions.

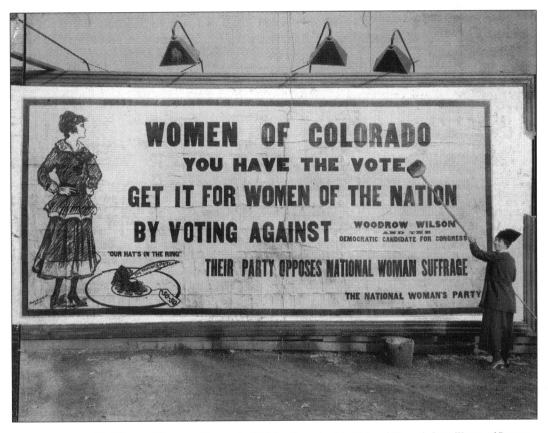

*Image courtesy of the Library of Congress, Manuscript Division, Records of the National Woman's Party Women of Protest: Photographs from the Records of the National Woman's Party*

1. What idea or object is being advertised? _____

2. Who paid for this billboard? _____

3. To what age group and gender does this billboard appeal? _____

_____

4. What is the obvious message on this billboard? _____

_____

5. What are the hidden messages on this billboard? _____

_____

6. In what ways is this billboard a healthy and/or unhealthy example of media? _____

_____

_____

# Early Billboards *(cont.)*

The political billboard below, created in 1948, is a campaign billboard.

**Directions:** Study the billboard. Match the correct letter to each number below.

*Image courtesy of The National Archives (187021)*

1. idea being advertised

a. bribery

2. audience

b. Gerald R. Ford, Jr. for U.S. Representative

3. obvious message

c. vote for Ford

4. method of advertising

d. adults of voting age

5. hidden message

e. Ford will address your concerns

# Billboards of Today

What billboards do you see every day in your city or town? Do you pass by without noticing them? Do you like looking at them?

**Directions:** Choose two billboards from your city. Sketch them in the spaces below and then answer the questions on page 40 for each billboard.

**Billboard One**

**Billboard Two**

# Billboards of Today *(cont.)*

**Directions:** Using the two billboards you sketched on page 39, complete this chart for each.

| Question | Billboard One | Billboard Two |
|---|---|---|
| 1. Who paid for this billboard? | | |
| 2. To what age group, economic group, and gender does this billboard appeal? | | |
| 3. What methods of advertising are used? | | |
| 4. What is the obvious message on this billboard? | | |
| 5. What are the hidden messages on this billboard? | | |
| 6. How is this billboard an example of healthy or unhealthy media? | | |

# Compare and Contrast

Think about billboards from the past and present. Can you see how this form of media has changed over the years?

**Directions:** Use encyclopedias, books, and the Internet to find a billboard made before 1970. Use search engine word terms such as *history of billboards*, *billboard ads*, and *early billboards*.

Draw the billboard you chose below.

# Compare and Contrast *(cont.)*

**Directions:** Look again at the drawing of one local billboard from your city. Compare it to the billboard you drew on page 41. Answer the questions below.

**1.** How are these two billboards different in terms of text?

_____

_____

**2.** How are these two billboards the same in terms of text?

_____

_____

**3.** How are these two billboards different in terms of images?

_____

_____

**4.** How are these two billboards the same in terms of images?

_____

_____

**5.** What methods of advertising are the same in the two billboards?

_____

_____

_____

**6.** What methods of advertising are different in the two billboards?

_____

_____

_____

**7.** How do you think billboards have changed over the years? Give some examples.

_____

_____

_____

_____

# Make a Billboard

Use what you've learned about billboards as a form of media! Follow the directions below to create your own billboard. You will need scrap paper, butcher paper (two sheets each, six feet long), transparent tape (one piece, six feet long), pencils with erasers, and markers or paint and brushes.

**Directions:** Get into groups of three or four. Discuss what your billboard will advertise. On scrap paper, draw what it will look like.

- Lay the pieces of butcher paper out on the floor. Put one above the other and tape them together at their longest end. You should now have a large rectangle.
- Draw the design for your billboard on the butcher paper. Make sure to add both pictures and text.
- Use markers or paint and brushes to add color to your billboard. Let it dry. Display it in a hallway or a classroom.

Once you have finished, answer the questions below about your billboard.

1. What product or idea does your billboard advertise?

   _____

2. What methods of advertising did you use?

   _____

   _____

3. What is the obvious message of your billboard?

   _____

   _____

   _____

4. What is the hidden message of your billboard, if any?

   _____

   _____

   _____

5. How is your billboard an example of healthy or unhealthy media?

   _____

   _____

   _____

   _____

# Radio

Radio has been around since the late part of the 19th century. Below are a few high points in radio history.

| | |
|---|---|
| **1887** ——→ | Scientist Heinrich Hertz discovers radio waves. |
| **1894** ——→ | Inventor Guglielmo Marconi forms the Wireless Telegraph and Signal Company. He was only 23 years old! |
| **1918** ——→ | Stations begin to broadcast news about politics. |
| **1919** ——→ | Companies make mass quantities of radio music boxes. |
| **1920** ——→ | KDKA begins broadcasts every night from 8:30–9:30 P.M. |
| **1922** ——→ | Over 500 stations begin broadcasting by the end of this year! |

*Photo from 1922 showing Asta Souvorina and her dog listening to the radio*

Image courtesy of the Library of Congress, Prints and Photographs Division (LC-USZ62-78074)

# Radio Ads

We use our eyes to study print ads. We use our ears to study radio ads. On the radio, we can't see pretty people who use toothpaste and shampoo. We can't see a child who likes one brand of oatmeal. People who make radio ads have to appeal to our sense of hearing.

**Directions:** Fill out the chart below. How can someone who makes radio ads use sound in methods of advertising? The first square of the chart has been done for you.

| Methods of Advertising | How it Works on the Radio |
|---|---|
| 1. Bandwagon | Have a crowd of happy people yell the name of one brand of peanut butter. |
| 2. Beautiful People | |
| 3. Fear | |
| 4. Warm and Fuzzy | |
| 5. Symbols | |
| 6. Humor | |
| 7. Testimonials | |
| 8. Repetition | |
| 9. Scientific Evidence | |

# Historic Radio Ads

The Internet lets you listen to all sorts of radio ads from the last century.

**Directions:** Use an Internet search engine. Find two radio ads by typing these key words into your search engine: *Old Radio Commercials*, *Historic Radio Commercials*, and *Radio Commercials from the 1930s, 1940s, and 1950s*. Once you have chosen two, deconstruct each commercial by filling in the sentences below. You can write out the sentences on a separate piece of paper.

1. This radio commercial is advertising _____

2. Sponsors including _____ paid for this radio commercial.

3. This radio commercial would appeal most to listeners who _____

   _____

   _____

4. In this radio commercial, sound is used as a persuasive technique in the following ways:

   _____

   _____

5. The obvious message of this radio commercial is that consumers should _____

   _____

   _____

   _____

6. The hidden message of this radio commercial is that the product will _____

   _____

   _____

   _____

7. This radio commercial is healthy or unhealthy because _____

   _____

   _____

   _____

   _____

   _____

# Today's Radio Ads

How have radio ads changed over the years? Have they become more or less clever? Shorter or longer? Funnier or more serious?

**Directions:** Listen to two commercials on the radio. You may listen to your radio at home, a classroom radio, or the radio on the Internet. Fill in the chart below.

| Questions | Ad One | Ad Two |
|---|---|---|
| 1. What product or idea is being advertised? | | |
| 2. Who paid for this radio ad? | | |
| 3. To what age group, economic group, and gender does this ad appeal? | | |
| 4. What methods of advertising are used in this ad? | | |
| 5. What is the obvious message in this ad? | | |
| 6. What are the hidden messages in this ad? | | |
| 7. In what ways is this ad a healthy or unhealthy example of media? | | |

# Record a Radio Ad

Now it's your turn to write and make a radio ad! You will need lined paper, a pen or pencil, and a tape recorder or computer with recording ability.

**Directions:** Get into a group of two-to-four students. Think of a product or idea you would like to sell. Decide how long to make your radio ad. Radio ads are usually quite short. They range from 15- and 30- to 60-second spots.

Write up a script for your ad, deciding who will play what parts. Will you need sound effects? Gather materials as needed and practice your ad.

Record your ad. You may need to record several takes. Once you are finished and happy with the ad, deconstruct it in one paragraph. In your paragraph, include the following points:

- your product
- your target audience
- techniques of persuasion
- type of lifestyle

- obvious messages
- hidden messages
- healthy or unhealthy media

_____

_____

_____

_____

_____

_____

_____

_____

_____

_____

_____

_____

_____

_____

_____

_____

_____

_____

Finally, play your radio commercial for your class!

# The First Radio Shows

In the 1930s and 1940s, people listened around the radio after dinner each night. They listened to Westerns such as "Hopalong Cassidy." They trembled at dramas such as "Cloak and Dagger." They laughed at funny shows like "Amos and Andy."

Libraries carry copies of these old radio shows and the Internet allows you to hear them, too.

**Directions:** Check out copies of two radio shows from the library. Or perform an Internet search to find two radio shows from before the 1950s. Type these key words into your search engine: *old time radio show*, *old radio*, and *radio lovers*.

Then, analyze and explain each radio show by filling in the blank spots in the conversation below and on page 50.

---

## Radio Show One

**Karen:** Hi, Marc, what's on the radio?

**Marc:** It's an old show called _____

**Karen:** What's it about?

**Marc:** It's about _____

_____

**Karen:** Who would be interested in that kind of a show?

**Marc:** Well, mostly people who _____

_____

**Karen:** What sound effects does the show use?

**Marc:** Oh, it uses _____

_____

**Karen:** Does this show have a message?

**Marc:** Sure! The message is that _____

_____

_____

---

# The First Radio Shows *(cont.)*

**Directions:** Describe the second radio show by filling in the blank spots in the dialogue below.

## Radio Show Two

**Kayla:** What are you listening to, Trent?

**Trent:** This? It's called _____

**Kayla:** I'm not sure it's a healthy show to listen to. Is it?

**Trent:** Actually, _____

_____

**Kayla:** Yes, but what's the message of the radio show?

**Trent:** If you listen carefully, you will hear that the message is _____

_____

**Kayla:** Okay. What sponsors does this show have?

**Trent:** Oh, there are ads for _____

_____

**Kayla:** There are lots of weird sounds in this show. How does the show use sound as a method of advertising?

**Trent:** Lots of things. To create a sense of _____ , the show uses _____ ,
and to create a sense of _____ , it uses _____

**Kayla:** So does this show appeal to boys or girls? And how old are the listeners, do you think?

**Trent:** I think the listeners are _____

_____

**Kayla:** Well, I'm going to have to listen to this show!

# War of the Worlds

In 1938, there was a young actor and director by the name of Orson Welles. He put a piece on the radio that scared people and made them feel ashamed.

It was the day before Halloween. Welles read a play based on H.G. Wells' famous novel called *The War of the Worlds*. It was a book about Martians who invade the Earth. Welles read one section that sounded like a news broadcast. It reported a Martian invasion.

The play sounded real. Listeners thought that Earth was being invaded by Mars. People tried to escape—cars jammed the roads. Other people hid in cellars. Some wrapped wet towels around their heads. They hoped to protect themselves from the Martians' poison gas.

**Directions:** Orson Welles' radio show caused panic. Listen to it on tapes from the library or listen to the broadcast on the Internet. Type these words into a search engine: *War of the Worlds radio* or *Orson Welles radio*, to find a link. When you have listened to part of the broadcast, answer the questions below.

| | |
|---|---|
| **1.** What is this story about? | |
| **2.** What parts of this radio show made people really think that Martians had come down to Earth? | |
| **3.** Do you think that the same panic could happen today from a radio show? Explain your answer. | |

# Radio Shows and Podcasts

Radio shows for children have been around for years and years. In the 1930s and 1940s, they lasted between 15 and 30 minutes. They always ended with a *cliffhanger*. A cliffhanger is an end that leaves the hero in trouble. This kind of end would make kids tune in the next day. They wanted to find out what happened to the Green Hornet, or Popeye the Sailor, or Chick Carter—Boy Detective.

Many radio stations around the world still air radio shows for young people. Now, children can also listen to podcasts created just for them. A podcast is a digital media file. You can download it and play it on your computer.

**Directions:** Use a radio or the Internet. Listen to two radio shows for young people. Answer the questions below and on the next page. To locate children's radio shows on the Internet, type the following words into a search engine: *children's radio shows, children's podcasts, radio for kids.*

| Questions | Radio Program One | Radio Program Two |
|---|---|---|
| 1. To what age group, economic group, and gender does this radio show appeal? | | |
| 2. What is the obvious message in this radio show? | | |
| 3. What are the hidden messages in this radio show? | | |
| 4. What are the methods of advertising in this show? | | |
| 5. Who sponsored this radio show—what commercials did you hear? | | |
| 6. In what ways is this radio show a healthy and/or unhealthy example of media? | | |

# Record a Radio Show

It's your turn to write and record a five- to ten-minute radio show. You will need several sheets of lined paper, a pen or pencil, a tape recorder or computer with recording capability, and materials to use for sound effects.

**Directions:** Get into a group of three or four students. Decide what format your radio show will take. Will you teach kids how to do something on your show, like playing the spoons or yodeling? Will you talk with guests like an unusual teacher or a parent who trains parrots? What ads will you have on your show?

Write up a script for your radio show and decide who will play what parts. Think about if you will need sound effects. Obtain materials as needed to create these sounds and practice the show.

Record your radio show—you may need to record several takes. When you are happy with the show, deconstruct it by filling in the chart below.

| | |
|---|---|
| Audience? | |
| Theme or Idea You're Promoting? | |
| Lifestyle Presented? | |
| How Do You Use Sound? | |
| Obvious Messages? | |
| Hidden Messages? | |
| Healthy or Unhealthy? | |

Finally, play your radio show for your class!

# Television

Television has a long and interesting history. Here are some of the highlights.

|  |  |
|---|---|
| **1862** | The first still image is transferred over wires. |
| **1876** | The term *cathode rays* is coined to describe the light emitted when an electric current is forced through a vacuum tube. |
| **1884** | Images are sent over wires using a rotating metal disk with 18 lines of resolution. |
| **1924/25** | Inventors sent mechanical transmissions of images over wire circuits. |
| **1927** | Bell Telephone and the U.S. Department of Commerce conduct the first long-distance use of television between Washington D.C. and New York City. |
| **1929** | The first television studio opened. |
| **1936** | About 200 television sets are in use across the world. |
| **1939** | The New York World's Fair demonstrates television and receivers. Some had to be coupled with a radio for sound. |
| **1948** | One million homes in the United States have television sets. |
| **1956** | The first remote control, called the Zenith Space Commander, is introduced. |
| **1966** | The first satellite carries television broadcasts internationally. |
| **1967** | Most television broadcasts are in color. |
| **1969** | 600 million people watch the first television transmission from the moon. |

*Inside a television studio, 1963*

Image courtesy of the Library of Congress, Prints and Photographs Division (LC-USZC2-4212)

# Your Television Journal

How important is television in your life?  Do you watch three hours a day?  Half an hour a day?  Do you only like a certain show or channel?

**Directions:**  For the next week, fill out the Television Journal below.  Be honest, there are no wrong answers!

| Date and Time | What I Watched | Length of Time I Watched |
|---|---|---|
| | | |
| | | |
| | | |
| | | |
| | | |
| | | |
| | | |

Do you not have a television in your house?  Write one page to explain why.  Add your opinions of television.  Would you prefer to have a television…or not?

# Television Ads

Television has shown ads since 1941. That year, the Federal Communications Commission allowed advertisement to appear on television.

NBC had a 10-second commercial for watches. The Bulova Watch Company paid the network seven dollars. Other stations also put ads on television for money.

In 1952, a television ad showed Mr. Potato Head®. The toy made $4 million in its first year. People saw that television advertising could be a very powerful media tool.

Many ads rely on a *jingle*. This is a catchy song. A jingle stays in the viewer's head after the ad is over. Some use cartoons to sell a thing or idea. Some create characters. These charaters star in different ads year after year.

Today, people watch about 40,000 television ads a year. Television ads are called the most important form of mass-market advertising.

# Classic Television Ads

Television ads have changed over the decades. At first a show might have just one ad that lasted a minute and a half. That's very long compared to the 15- or 30-second ads we see on television today.

**Directions:** Using the Internet, view two ads that aired in the 1950s, 1960s, or 1970s. Type the words *classic commercials*, *old commercials*, or *television commercials* into your favorite search engine. In the space below, describe each ad in the form of a short essay. Make sure to note the following items in your description.

- Who paid for this ad?
- To what group does it appeal?
- What methods of advertising are used?

- What hidden and obvious messages exist?
- How is this ad healthy or unhealthy media?

# Today's Television Ads

How have television ads changed? To begin with, ads for cigarettes have been banned since the 1970s. Ads for alcohol exist, but they are not allowed to show people actually drinking alcohol.

We see more ads now than we did in the 1960s. Then, an hour-long television program in the United States would be made up of 51 minutes of a television show, and nine minutes of ads. Now, a typical television show runs 42 minutes, with 18 minutes of ads! What else about television advertising has changed?

**Directions:** View two television ads at home or at school. Describe each by answering the questions below.

| Question | Commercial One | Commercial Two |
|---|---|---|
| Who paid for this television ad? | | |
| Would this ad appeal to boys, girls, or both? | | |
| What age group would like this ad? | | |
| What methods of advertising are used? | | |
| What is the obvious message in this ad? | | |
| What is the hidden message in this commercial? | | |
| In what way is this ad a healthy or unhealthy form of media? | | |

Now describe what you noticed about these ads of today. What is interesting about them? What do you like? What do you dislike?

_____

_____

_____

_____

_____

# Compare and Contrast

Now that you have viewed at least four television commercials—two from the past, and two from the present—think about how they have changed over time.

**Directions:** In the space below, complete a Venn diagram to show how past and present commercials differ. Also, explain how they are similar. You might want to show how people or products have changed, and comment on music, scenery, pacing, or voices.

In the circle on the left, write features of the commercials from the past. In the circle on the right, write features of the commercials from the present. Where the two circles overlap, write features that are common to both commercials.

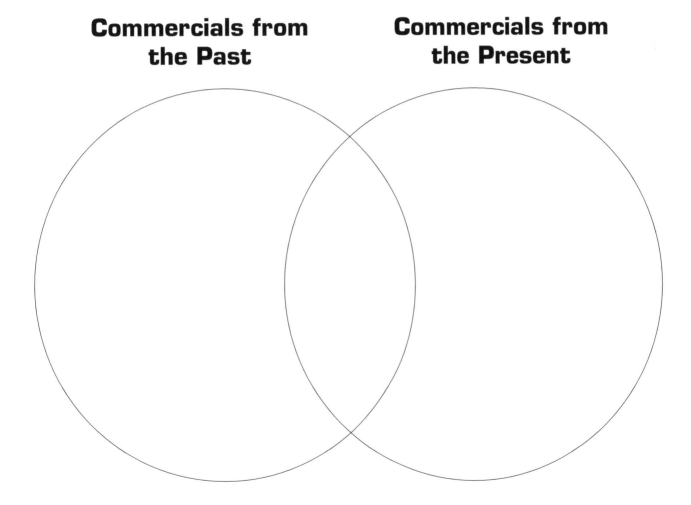

**Commercials from the Past**

**Commercials from the Present**

# Create a Television Ad

Get inspired to film your own television ad!  You will need several sheets of lined paper, a pen or pencil, a video recorder or computer with video recording capability, and costumes and props.

**Directions:**  In a group of three or four, decide what product you will sell on your television ad.  Will you tell a story?  Sing a song?  Do a dance?  How will you get people to buy your product?

Write a script for your ad.  Decide who will play what parts, and who will be the director and actors.  Find costumes and props.  See the script below for how to write your ad.

---

### Sample Script

**Mr. Mudrick** (walks into kitchen looking mad):  Why can't I find any of my socks?

**His Son** (feeding pet dog):  Maybe Spot ate them.

**Mr. Mudrick** (looks into dog's mouth):  If only there was some way to keep my socks together.

---

Once it is written, practice your ad until you are happy with it.  Record your commercial—you may need to record several takes.

Describe your commercial below using these questions.

1.  What product or idea does your ad sell?

   _____

2.  Who is your target audience?

   _____

3.  What methods of advertising do you use?

   _____

   _____

4.  What messages exist in your commercial?

   _____

   _____

5.  How is your television ad an example of healthy or unhealthy media?

   _____

   _____

   _____

Finally, pop some popcorn and play your television commercial for your class!

# Television News

All over the world, people wake up to the morning news on television. Some come home from work or school and turn on the news. The news has been on television since 1948. Reporters have talked about wars and sports. They have covered elections and grand openings, health problems, and human-interest stories.

Some people say that television news is too violent. It uses scary stories to get people to tune in. "If it bleeds, it leads." This sentence shows how television news begins with the most exciting story.

**Directions:** Watch the first five minutes of three different news programs on television. Record your findings on the chart below. The first one has been done for you.

| Name of News Program | Topic of Lead Story | Description of Lead Story |
|---|---|---|
| KVRW News at Night | A car was stolen | Two young men stole an older man's car from the parking lot of a local market and then tried to shoot him. |
| | | |
| | | |
| | | |
| | | |

# Healthy Television News?

How does what you see on television news affect you?  Which stories are healthy forms of media?  Which are unhealthy?

**Directions:**  Watch one half-hour of news on television.  Fill out the chart below, following the example.

**Name of news program watched:** _____

| Topic | Description | Healthy or Unhealthy? |
|---|---|---|
| Child saves her grandmother | A three-year-old called 911 after her grandma fell and couldn't get up.  Doctors then saved the grandmother. | Healthy.  This is a piece that makes people feel good because it has a happy ending. |
|  |  |  |
|  |  |  |
|  |  |  |
|  |  |  |
|  |  |  |

# The Role of Sponsors

Sponsors are people or companies who pay television stations to put their ads on the air.

Have you ever noticed that ads for toys run while cartoons are on television? Ads for cars and trucks air during football games on television. Ads for makeup and health products run during soap operas.

Sponsors are smart. They study who watches what programs on television. Then, they place their ads right where their target audiences will see them!

**Directions:** To better understand the role of sponsors, watch a half-hour television program at home or at school. Take notes on what products you see advertised in the space below. Then, answer the questions.

**Name of Television Program:** _____

## Products Advertised:

- _____
- _____
- _____
- _____
- _____
- _____
- _____

1. To what age, economic, and gender groups does this television program appeal?

_____

_____

_____

2. What products were advertised most often?

_____

_____

_____

3. Why did the advertiser choose these products for this program?

_____

_____

_____

# Hidden Messages in TV

Now you understand how to find the obvious messages in media. You also know how to find the hidden messages. Put your skills into practice!

**Directions:** Review the television program you watched for the assignment on page 63. Or, you can watch another half-hour television program if you would prefer. In the space below, list all of the obvious messages in the program. Then, list all of the hidden messages you see in the program. List hidden and obvious messages in the ads as well.

| Obvious Messages | Hidden Messages |
| --- | --- |
|  |  |

# Turn Off Your Television

Kids in the United States watch about 1,023 hours of television each year. Television can teach people about history and sports, art and nature. But too much watching can lead to poor health.

National TV-Turnoff Week began in 1994. Its founders hope to show the negative effects of watching television. Each year, thousands of people turn off their televisions for a week.

The next few activities will help you to try your own TV-Turnoff Week.

**Directions:** Complete the exercises below to understand your relationship to television.

1. Rate the importance of television in your life. A rating of 1 means that television is not important at all while 10 means that it is very important.

   _____

2. Now, explore a group that is part of this national move to turn off your television. Using the Internet, type the following words into your search engine: *TV turnoff, turn off your television, television turnoff.* Study the home page of one group's website and fill in the chart below.

| | |
|---|---|
| **a.** Who paid for this website? | |
| **b.** To what age group, economic group, and gender does this homepage appeal? | |
| **c.** What methods of advertising are used on this homepage? | |
| **d.** What are the obvious messages on this homepage? | |
| **e.** What are the hidden messages on their home page? | |
| **f.** In what ways is this homepage a healthy or unhealthy example of media? | |

# No TV?  What to Do?

What do you do when you're not watching television?  Do you play soccer, build go-carts, or take acting classes?  What would you do if you had to give up your favorite television show?  Would you learn to draw?  Make a short film?  Train your puppy?

**Directions:**  Alone, or in groups of two or three, think of 20 activities that kids can do instead of watching television.  Write them in the spaces below.

## Alternatives to Television

1. _____

2. _____

3. _____

4. _____

5. _____

6. _____

7. _____

8. _____

9. _____

10. _____

11. _____

12. _____

13. _____

14. _____

15. _____

16. _____

17. _____

18. _____

19. _____

20. _____

**Boys playing basketball, 1911**

**Children's playground, 1926**

*Images courtesy of the Library of Congress, Prints and Photographs Division (LC-USZ62-71329 and LC-USZ62-47700)*

# TV-Turnoff Week Journal

**Directions:** For the next week, try to watch little or no television. Keep a journal in the space below. Write down how you felt every day about not watching television. Write down what you did instead.

## JOURNAL

Day One

_____
_____
_____

Day Two

_____
_____
_____

Day Three

_____
_____
_____

Day Four

_____
_____
_____

Day Five

_____
_____
_____

Day Six

_____
_____
_____

Day Seven

_____
_____
_____

# Music

People hear music almost as soon as they are born. You grew up hearing songs like "Itsy Bitsy Spider" and "Three Blind Mice." Now, you probably have a favorite band and a favorite song.

Music is an important part of our life. It is also a form of media that surrounds us every day.

**Directions:** Complete the sentences below to study your relationship to music.

1. My favorite type of music is _____

   _____

2. My favorite song is _____

   _____

3. My favorite singer is _____

   _____

4. I like to listen to music when I am _____

   _____

5. I do not like to listen to music when I am _____

   _____

6. When I am in a bad mood, music _____

   _____

7. When I am in a good mood, music _____

   _____

# Conflicts in Music

Sometimes music creates conflict. Below are some examples.

- In the 1950s, kids sent letters to a Chicago radio station. They asked the station to stop playing rhythm and blues. They called these songs "dirty music."

- In the 1960s, a Texas radio station stopped playing all of Bob Dylan's records. They said that they couldn't understand his words. They thought his songs might be obscene.

- In the 1980s, people formed the Parents Resource Music Center. They urged producers to rate new albums as healthy or unhealthy for kids.

- In the early 21st century, people attacked rap singer Eminem. Critics said that his songs were violent.

"File sharing" is one of the main conflicts in the early 21st century. File sharing means a listener can buy a piece of music and put it on a computer. Then other people can hear this music. They can record it for free instead of buying it at the store.

**Directions:** To understand the conflict about file sharing, answer the questions below.

1. How would you as a listener benefit from file sharing? How might it hurt you?

_____

_____

_____

2. How would you as a musician benefit from people sharing your music? How might file sharing hurt you?

_____

_____

_____

Now, think about a recent music conflict you have heard of or read about. Describe it in the space below. If you need help, look at magazines, newspapers, and the Internet.

_____

_____

_____

_____

_____

# Analyze a Song

Lots of people listen to a song and only hear the instruments. Sometimes, they don't pay attention to the lyrics. But the words to a song are as important as the drums, bass, and guitars.

**Directions:** Choose your favorite song. Write down the lyrics on the back of this page. Then, answer the questions.

1. What is this song about?

   _____

   _____

   _____

2. To what age group and gender does this song appeal?

   _____

   _____

3. What are the obvious messages of this song?

   _____

   _____

   _____

   _____

4. What are the hidden messages of this song?

   _____

   _____

   _____

   _____

5. In what ways is this song a healthy or unhealthy example of media?

   _____

   _____

   _____

   _____

   _____

   _____

# Music Videos

One form of music media is videos. Music videos are two-to-three minute movies. Bands make them to go with a song. The first short music videos appeared on television in the 1980s. Now, many bands record at least one music video for every hit song or album they put out.

**Directions:** You can analyze a music video as a form of media. Read the screenplay of the short video below and then answer the questions.

---

**Fade in:**
Shows a new girl at school sitting by herself in the cafeteria. She looks lonely and sad. Two other girls in school uniforms appear. They see the new girl and walk toward her with a stuffed kitten toy.

**Band appears**
Standing in the cafeteria. They are all beautiful women, dressed in pink and light blue. They smile as they play their instruments and sing.

**Song**
*"If you're feeling lost and lonely,*
*not a friend for miles to see,*
*you can sit at my big table*
*and share a laugh with me."*

**Pan in:**
The new girl's face is happy now. She holds her head high and cradles the stuffed kitten with a smile.

**Close-up:**
All three girls sit at the table together. They talk and laugh.

---

1. Who would enjoy this music video? _____

2. What techniques of persuasion do you find in this video? _____

3. How would you describe the two different lifestyles presented in this video? Which is more glamorous?

   _____

   _____

4. What is the obvious message in this video?

   _____

   _____

5. Do you think there is a hidden message in this video? If so, describe it.

   _____

   _____

6. In what ways is this video a healthy or unhealthy example of media?

   _____

   _____

# Music Videos *(cont.)*

Music videos use symbols and hidden messages. They use beautiful people and other methods of advertising. They are just like any form of media.

**Directions:** Study your favorite music video. Watch the video, and take notes. Then, pretend you are a music critic for a magazine or newspaper. Write a review of this music video. In your report, note the following:

- band name
- name of song in video
- who would like this video

- obvious message
- hidden message
- healthy or unhealthy example of media

DAILY TRIBUNE

# Make a Music Video

Now that you understand what goes into a music video, it is time to make one of your own! You will need several sheets of lined paper, a pen or pencil, a video recorder or computer with video recording capability, and costumes and props.

**Directions:** In a group of five or six, decide what song you will use. Will you make a video for someone else's song? Or will you come up with your own song and create a music video for it?

Write up a script for your video. Decide who will play what parts. Decide on a director, actors, and band members/singers, if needed. Decide if you will need costumes and props and get the materials as needed.

Practice your music video until you are happy with it, then record it. You may need to record several takes. You can switch back and forth between filming your band members/singers and filming your actors.

When you have finished recording the music video, answer the questions below.

1. What is your music video about? _____

   _____

2. Who is your target audience? _____

   _____

3. What methods of advertising do you use in this video? _____

   _____

   _____

4. What obvious messages exist in your video? _____

   _____

   _____

5. What hidden messages, if any, exist in your video? _____

   _____

   _____

6. In what ways is your music video an example of healthy or unhealthy media? _____

   _____

   _____

   _____

   _____

Finally, play your music video for your class!

# Videogames

People have played videogames since the 1970s. The first arcade videogame was called *Computer Space*. *Space Invaders*, *PacMan*, and *Centipede* showed up in arcades. In 1972, people began to play videogames on their own televisions. Kids played games like *Pong*, which had simple lines and circles. These were games that required a large joystick.

These days, videogames let players enter great worlds. Games have colorful images and sounds. The console—that is, the actual game box—has changed, too.

**Directions:** Study the picture of the videogame console from the 1970s. Look at the picture of a recent videogame console. Explain in a few sentences how these consoles have changed, then answer the remaining questions.

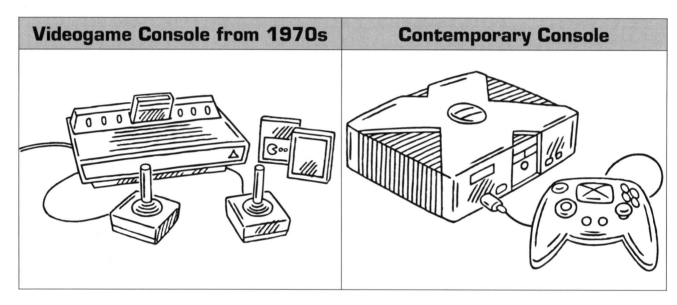

| Videogame Console from 1970s | Contemporary Console |

1. How have these consoles changed? _____

_____

_____

2. Why do you think people like to play videogames? _____

_____

3. How often do you play videogames? _____

_____

4. What is your favorite videogame? Why? _____

_____

5. If you do not play videogames, explain why. _____

_____

_____

# Videogame Ads

People who make ads for videogames know that their pictures and words must be exciting. They know that videogame players like vivid graphics. They must get people to choose their game over hundreds of others!

**Directions:** Study this print advertisement for a videogame and then answer the questions.

1. What is the name of this videogame? _____

2. What company makes this videogame? _____

3. What is this company's slogan? _____

4. What is the obvious message of this print ad? _____

_____

5. What is the hidden message of this print ad? _____

_____

6. In what ways is this ad a healthy or unhealthy form of media? _____

_____

# Videogame Ads *(cont.)*

Use what you have learned so far to analyze one videogame ad.

**Directions:** Locate an ad for a videogame. This may be a print ad from a newspaper or magazine. It may be a television ad or on an Internet website. Then, answer the questions below.

| | |
|---|---|
| **1.** What is the name of this videogame? | |
| **2.** What slogan does this advertisement use? | |
| **3.** Who paid for this ad? | |
| **4.** To what age group, economic group, and gender does this ad appeal? | |
| **5.** What obvious messages exist in this ad? | |
| **6.** What hidden messages can you find in this ad? | |
| **7.** In what ways is this ad an example of healthy or unhealthy media? | |

# Violence in Videogames

Throwing bananas at apes!  Shooting zombies!  Wrestling wizards!  In 1998, 80 percent of kids' favorite videogames showed some sort of injury or death.

Most people who play videogames see these images.  In one game, a player runs down people on the street.  Players who finish this game end up "killing" a lot of people.

**Directions:**  Think about a videogame you like.  Is it violent?  Why do you like it more than others?  Complete the sentences below.

1.  My favorite videogame is _____.

2.  The point of this videogame is to _____

   _____

   _____.

3.  I like this videogame in particular because _____

   _____

   _____.

   _____

4.  This videogame could be considered violent because _____

   _____

   _____.

   _____

5.  My feelings about violence in the real world are _____

   _____

   _____

   _____.

6.  My feelings about violence in videogames are _____

   _____.

   _____

   _____.

7.  I think many people my age like/dislike violent videogames because _____

   _____

   _____.

# Your Body and Feelings

When you play videogames, what do you notice about your body? What do you notice about your feelings? Does anything change?

**Directions:** Play a videogame for 10 minutes. You may choose to do this on a class computer. Or you may play at home, at a friend's house, or at an arcade. Then, answer the questions below.

1. What game did you play? _____

   _____

2. What was the point of the videogame? _____

   _____

   _____

3. How did your body change when you played? (Did your heart pound? Did your head hurt? Did you feel full of energy? Did your hands sweat?) _____

   _____

4. How did your feelings change when you played? (Did you feel happy? Angry? Tense? Excited?)

   _____

   _____

Now, play 10 more minutes of a videogame. Notice again the changes in your body and feelings. Answer the questions below.

5. How is this videogame violent, if at all? _____

   _____

   _____

6. Did playing this game make you feel angry? Explain your answer. _____

   _____

   _____

7. Do you think that violence is okay in videogames? Explain your answer. _____

   _____

   _____

# Your Favorite Videogame

Now you understand videogames as a form of media. Look at one game in depth.

**Directions:** Choose your favorite videogame to analyze. Pretend you are writing a review of it for your favorite gaming magazine. Remember that a review is not just a summary. It uses creative details to show a reader what something is actually like. In your review, make sure to note the following details:

- brand name and name of videogame
- who will enjoy the game
- what type of world you enter into through this game
- how techniques of persuasion are used in this game
- the obvious and hidden messages in this game
- whether you believe this game to be a healthy or unhealthy form of media

# Videogame Debate

You have learned that videogames cause conflict. A classroom debate will help you to decide how you feel about this popular form of media. For the debate you will need encyclopedias and the Internet, several sheets of paper, pencils or pens, and a wristwatch or clock with a second hand.

**Directions:** Form two groups. One group will speak in support of videogames. The other will speak against them.

In your group, debate the topics below. Use encyclopedias and the Internet to do research on each topic. For instance, if you want to study the effects of videogames and violence, type these words into a search engine or look for them under *videogames* in your encyclopedia. Write down any arguments you have to support your position on videogames. For instance, for violence, if you are in favor of these games, you might argue that playing them keeps kids busy so kids don't get into fights.

If you are against violence in videogames, you might say that playing makes kids angry and more likely to fight.

Use facts. This will help you make your point.

When you have researched the topics, spend a little time rehearsing what you will say during the debate. Practice with someone else in your group asking them to pretend to be from the opposing group.

---

### Debate Topics

- violence
- homework
- relationships with family and friends
- effects on body and feelings

---

Now that your group has gathered their thoughts, it is time to debate. Choose one person—an adult works well in this role—to be the moderator. Choose one person from each group to be the speaker for the first topic. Select a group to go first through a coin toss.

The moderator calls out a topic. The speaker from the first group has one minute to make an argument. At the end of the minute, the speaker from the second group has a minute to debate the opposite view.

Select another person from your group to speak about the next topic. Now the second group goes first. The speaker has one minute to present his or her views, and so on. Be sure to leave five minutes at the end so that both groups can talk about videogames as a whole.

# Packaging

So many things come in packages. When you wake up, you reach for a carton of milk or a box of oatmeal. These are packages. A tube of toothpaste is a package. So is a jar of peanut butter and a bag of store-bought bread.

Packages are a form of media. We see them every day. They give us clues about what is inside a container. They also help us to decide whether or not we want the product.

Here are a few details that people think about when they create a new package:

| | |
|---|---|
| • shape | • slogan |
| • color | • graphics |
| • pictures | • name |
| • text | • font |
| • size | |

In the 16th century, sellers began to wrap their products in paper. They wrote the product's name on the outside of the package. By the 1700s, people sold groceries in bottles or jars. They glued labels to the outside. Today, machines print out thousands of candy bar labels at a time. But back in history, each label was made by hand. In fact, people even made the jars by hand!

# Packages of the Past

Packages have been around for hundreds of years. What did they look like back then?

*Image courtesy of the Library of Congress, Prints and Photographs Division (LC-USZ62-4623)*

**Directions:** Study this package label for glue, created in 1860. Look up the word "unrivalled." Write the definition in the space below:

Unrivalled = _____

Now, copy the correct phrase from the Phrase Bank into each blank space below.

1. This package was paid for by _____.

2. This package would appeal to _____.

3. The obvious message of this package is _____

   _____.

4. The hidden message of this package is _____

   _____.

5. The methods of advertising on this package are _____

   _____.

---

## Phrase Bank

this glue will bond your family together

Dr. Spaulding & Co.

plain folks, warm and fuzzy, and hyperbole

this buckskin glue is unrivalled

people who need glue for projects

---

# Packages of Today

Packages are all around us. You can study what a package designer wants you to think or feel anytime you see a box, carton, tube, bottle, or can.

**Directions:** Choose your favorite package label to study. Draw it in the space below. Then, answer the questions.

1. Who paid for this package? _____

2. What gender, economic group, and age group does this package appeal to? _____

3. What obvious message do you see in this package? _____

4. What hidden message do you see in this package? _____

5. In what ways is this package a healthy or unhealthy example of media? _____

_____

# Color, Shape, and Words

What color should you make a box for a stereo? Should a box of thumbtacks be square or circular? How many words should you put on a package for a doll? People who make packages must ask themselves these questions.

**Directions:** Study the package facts below. Then, answer the questions using full sentences.

## Design Facts

- Buyers feel calm when they see the color blue.
- The colors red, yellow, and orange make buyers feel hungry.
- The color green makes buyers think of the Earth.
- Buyers find mystery in the color purple.
- Buyers want to buy a product if the package has lots of information on it.
- Buyers like packages with strange shapes.
- Cartoon and superhero characters on packages appeal to children.

## Questions

1. What color would you make a package that holds a ping-pong table that needs to be put together?

   _____

2. What package shape might you create for a kids' cereal to make it stand out to buyers?

   _____

3. What color would you make a box for a beach towel made from recycled tennis shoes?

   _____

4. What color would you make a box that holds a pretend crystal ball?

   _____

5. What image would you put on a package that holds children's pajamas?

   _____

6. What color might you make a box that holds a candy bar?

   _____

7. What kind of information would you put on a box of cough syrup?

   _____

# Compare and Contrast

You have looked at packages from the past and present. Now, study them to see how they have changed over the centuries.

**Directions:** Examine each package on page 86. Answer the questions below and complete the essay assignment.

## Label One

1. What is this product? What is the brand name? _____

   _____

2. What stands out about the text on this package label? _____

   _____

3. What stands out about the image on this package label? _____

   _____

4. What does this package label promise buyers? _____

   _____

5. What slogan does this package use? _____

   _____

## Label Two

6. What is this product? What is the brand name? _____

   _____

7. What stands out about the text on this package label? _____

   _____

8. What stands out about the image on this package label? _____

   _____

9. What does this package label promise buyers? _____

   _____

10. What slogan does this package use? _____

    _____

11. You have seen how packages have changed over the centuries. You have also seen that some parts of packages remain the same. On a separate piece of paper, write a short essay comparing and contrasting packages from the past and present. As you write your essay, pay attention to the words, images, slogans, promises, and brand names.

**Label One**

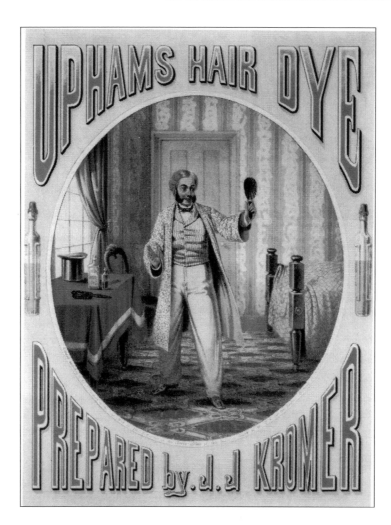

*Image courtesy of the Library of Congress, Prints and Photographs Division (LC-USZ62-4630)*

**Label Two**

# Design a Package

You know now that the makers of packages pay attention to words, images, slogans, brands, and colors. Using this information, design a package of your own. It can be a box, can, bottle, tube, or carton. You will need scratch paper, a pencil with an eraser, one piece of large construction paper, glue or tape, and markers or colored pencils.

**Directions**

1. Decide what product you will package. Sketch your idea for a package on scratch paper. Think of a brand name, a slogan, words, images, and anything else you think will help to sell your product.

2. Decide on a size, color (or colors), and shape for your package.

3. Make your package out of construction paper. Fold your package into a three-dimensional shape (follow steps A–H or I and II below) and glue or tape it.

4. Draw words and images, brand name and slogan on your package with markers or colored pencils.

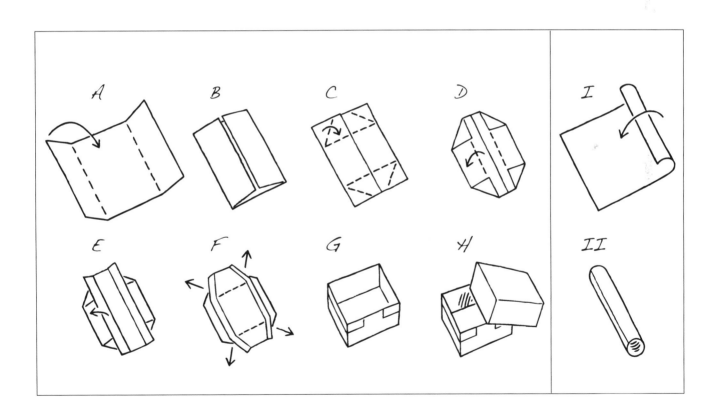

# Product Placement

Have you ever watched a person eat one brand of potato chips on a television show? Have you opened a book for kids to find images of one brand of cookies? Have you watched a dog in the movies play basketball with a ball that has a logo on it? These are all forms of product placement.

Product placement happens when a brand-name item appears in some form of media. Here are some examples:

- a character in your favorite television show is always wearing Levi's® shorts
- the song "Take Me Out to the Ball Game" mentions buying Cracker Jacks®
- a picture book that teaches kids to count uses pictures of Oreos®
- your favorite videogame asks you to take characters to Kentucky Fried Chicken®
- the main characters in your favorite movie use Apple® laptop computers

How is product placement different from an ad?

An ad gives us an obvious message—you need this product.

A product placed in a movie, book, song, television show, or videogame has a hidden message. Sellers hope that we will buy something just because we've seen it in one of these forms of media.

# Product Placement in Action

Sellers hope that placing a product will look natural in a television show or movie. Then people will take an interest in a brand name without realizing that they have seen it!

There are three ways to place a product:

1. It just happens. An actor, a director, or a set decorator decides to use a brand-name product. This makes movies, television, and other forms of media look more real. Can you relate more to a character who is eating from a carton marked "Ice Cream," or more to one who scoops from a carton marked with a brand-name?

2. Product placement may be a trade. A movie director promises to put one brand of candy bar in a film. The seller promises to give candy bars to the cast and crew.

3. Product placement is purchased. The seller of one type of cat food pay a television producer money to make sure that the main character in the show eats this brand of cat food.

**Directions:** On television or on the Internet, watch a movie preview. It should be no longer than three minutes. You can find hundreds of previews by typing the words *movie trailer* into a search engine. In the space below, write down every brand-name product you see in the preview.

**Name of movie being previewed** _____

**Products placed within the preview** _____

_____

_____

_____

_____

_____

_____

_____

_____

_____

_____

_____

_____

_____

_____

# Products in Books

Many books for kids show product placement. Six-year-olds learn to read and count by looking at pictures of brand-name candies and cookies in books made just for them.

**Directions:** Study these pages from a kids' alphabet book and then answer the questions.

1. What product is placed in this book? _____

   _____

2. Who paid for this product to be placed in this book?

   _____

3. What gender, economic group, and age group does this book target?

   _____

   _____

4. What obvious message do you see in this book?

   _____

   _____

5. What hidden message do you see in this book?

   _____

   _____

6. In what ways is this book an example of healthy or unhealthy media?

   _____

   _____

# Products in Videogames

In the 1980s, products showed up in videogames. One game from 1989 had a pizza chain. Another game showed a cartoon figure from a soft drink. The bananas in one game have stickers with a brand name on them.

Games of today show fast food restaurants. They show brand-name cell phones. They also show candy and soda.

**Directions:** Answer the questions below. This will help you to understand why products are placed in videogames.

1. Why do you think sellers want to put their products in videogames? _____

   _____

   _____

2. Why do you think videogame designers agree to put name-brand products in their games?

   _____

   _____

3. Do you think players like or dislike product placement in videogames? Explain your answer.

   _____

   _____

4. How do you think players feel when they see brand-name products in their videogames?

   _____

   _____

Now you get to think like a videogame designer. Make up a game. In the space below, draw a scene from your game. Add at least three examples of product placement. Make sure to write the name of each brand on your product.

# Products on Television

Many television programs for children place products like toys and candy. Sellers hope kids will see and buy these products.

**Directions:** Choose a kids' television program that is 30 to 60 minutes in length. Watch the program and see how many name-brand products you can find. Write them down in the space below and explain how they are used.

For example, you might write

*In this television show, Sandy wears Slapstick-brand jeans and uses a SmartRite computer. Sandy drinks Rockin' Cola and eats Tatertoes potato chips.*

Pay attention to brand-name clothing, shoes, hats, food and drink, computers and videogames, cell phones, stores, restaurants, sports equipment, and toys.

# Taste Test!

Does name brand bottled water taste better than tap water? Or do we simply believe what sellers tell us? Hold a blind taste-test to find out which water you like best. You will need a liter bottle of name-brand bottled water, a liter bottle of tap water, two brown paper grocery bags, scissors, masking tape, a pen, small paper cups (two for each student), scrap paper (one small piece for each student), and a receptacle for scrap paper (a bowl, hat, or paper bag).

**Directions:**

1.  Choose one person, preferably the teacher, to be the tester. Cut bags to fit around each liter bottle. Tape them so no one can read the labels on the bottles. On one bottle, write *Water #1*. On the other, write *Water #2*.

2.  Line up for a taste test. Everyone but the first student should remain five feet away from the tester. The tester pours a little water from the first bottle into one cup and a little water from the second bottle into a second cup. The student should then drink both samples, comparing them in his or her mind.

3.  When the student has tasted both kinds of water, he or she should write down the preferred bottle, #1 or #2, on a piece of scrap paper, fold it, then put it in the bowl or bag. Do not discuss your taste test with other students!

4.  When everyone has finished tasting the water, tally up students' preferences. Then, take the labels off of the water bottles. Discuss the following questions with your class:

    *   Were you surprised by which water the class preferred?

    *   What were the differences between the two types of water in terms of taste?

    *   Why might someone choose to buy name-brand water over generic water?

    *   Why might someone choose to buy generic water over name-brand water?

    *   How do you think product placement affects students?

# Products in Movies

You have studied product placement in television shows. You can also study and chart the placement of products in a movie.

**Directions:** Choose a movie. Watch it carefully. Take notes on how many brand-name products you can find.

Write down the products in the space below. Explain how they are used. For example, you might write:

> *In the movie, "Sixth Graders On the Run," Josh and Raul wear Speedster track shoes and jerseys. They drink Get-Up-and-Go sports drinks and eat Nutty-Chew energy bars.*

Pay attention to brand-name clothing, shoes, hats, food and drink, computers and videogames, cell phones, stores, restaurants, sports equipment, and toys.

_____

_____

_____

_____

_____

_____

_____

_____

_____

_____

_____

_____

_____

_____

_____

_____

_____

_____

_____

_____

# Magazines

There are thousands of magazines. Each of them is a form of media.

Magazines for kids first appeared in the United States in the mid-1900s. Now, they are all over the world.

Different magazines cover different topics. Some publish stories and photos about music. Some cover television and movies. Some focus on pets. Some magazines are about sports or cars.

Girls most often buy lifestyle magazines. These magazines cover clothes, travel, sports, movie stars, and other general topics. Many boys buy magazines about sports such as biking or backpacking. Both boys and girls are affected by the pictures they see in magazines.

*Image courtesy of the Library of Congress, Prints and Photographs Division (LC-USZ62-131651)*

**Directions:** Study this magazine cover from 1914 and then answer the questions below.

1. What is the name of this magazine? _____

2. To what gender and age group does this magazine cover appeal? _____

3. What is the obvious message of this magazine cover? _____

   _____

4. What is the hidden message of this magazine cover? _____

   _____

# Tricks in Photography

That berry pie looks perfect on the front cover of a magazine. You try the recipe, but your pie comes out leaking and lopsided. That female runner looks pretty in the magazine photo. But when you run, you look sweaty and breathless.

Magazine photographers use all sorts of tricks so that their photos look good. Here are a few of their methods:

Image courtesy of the Library of Congress, Prints and Photographs Division (LC-DIG-ppmsca-02941)

- How does a turkey dinner look picture-perfect in a cooking magazine? A food stylist may spray the food with a mixture of water and corn syrup. This adds shine and appeal.

- How does a magazine cover show a pie still steaming from the oven? Magazine photographers soak cotton balls in water. Then they microwave them and put them out of sight behind the pie. This creates steam.

- How can that cover model with the clear skin and blond hair be so handsome? In reality, the man could have acne and dull brown hair. Magazine photographers can alter pictures so that skin looks clear. On the computer, they can even change someone's hair color from brown to blond!

- How did your favorite actor get so fat so fast on the cover of the magazine in the grocery store? Photographers can put an actor's head on another person's body. This adds drama to a story and makes people want to buy a copy of the magazine.

- Did that surfer really ride the giant wave on the cover of the sports magazine? Maybe, maybe not. Photographers can combine two photos—one of a surfer, and one of a huge wave—to make it look like one amazing photo.

Image courtesy of the Library of Congress, Prints and Photographs Division (LC-USZC4-12222)

# Tricks in Photography (cont.)

Now that you understand how photographers can change an image, study the effects of these tricks on people who look at these photos.

**Directions:** Read each scene. Circle the letter or letters that best explain what might happen after someone sees a photo.

1. A young man wants chest muscles like the men he sees in the sports magazines. He works out at the gym three times a week, but he still doesn't look like the models. At last, he

   **a.** stops going to the gym and just plays videogames.
   **b.** goes to the gym seven days a week and eats only carrots.
   **c.** realizes that he cannot look like that so decides to exercise regularly but not to worry.
   **d.** none of the above

2. Two kids see beautiful cupcakes on the cover of a cooking magazine. They make the recipe for Mother's Day, but their cupcakes turn out lopsided and funny looking. The kids

   **a.** throw their cupcakes in the trash and buy some at a bakery.
   **b.** give their mother the cupcakes knowing they tried hard and made them with love.
   **c.** make another batch and feel sad when these look only a little nicer.
   **d.** none of the above.

3. A girl who is having trouble with acne reads magazines with photos of beautiful women with clear skin. She

   **a.** tries to take care of her skin the best she can and just hopes it clears up soon.
   **b.** buys thick makeup to cover her acne.
   **c.** feels ugly and hides behind her long hair.
   **d.** none of the above.

4. A boy without much money sees a magazine ad. In it, two guys wear brand-name jeans and are surrounded by pretty girls. The boy

   **a.** gets a job and saves his money so he can afford the jeans.
   **b.** feels like he will never have a girlfriend because he can't afford the brand-name jeans.
   **c.** tries to steal jeans from the store and gets caught.
   **d.** none of the above.

# Magazines for Children

You can compare and contrast two magazines for kids. This will help you to become a smart reader of this important type of media.

**Directions:** Choose one magazine from the first list. Choose another magazine from the second list. You may choose to compare these magazines in print form or on the Internet.

| List One | | List Two | |
|---|---|---|---|
| Teen Voices | Cat Fancy | Seventeen | Girls' Life |
| Skipping Stones | Dog Fancy | YM | Elle Girl |
| The Writer's Slate | New Moon Publishing | National Geographic Kids | Teen Vogue |
| Boys' Life | Cobblestone | CosmoGirl! | American Girl |

Now, fill out the chart below.

| Question | Magazine One | Magazine Two |
|---|---|---|
| What is the name of this magazine? | | |
| What age group and gender will be interested in this magazine? | | |
| What are the obvious messages in this magazine? | | |
| What are the hidden messages in this magazine? | | |
| What methods of advertising are used in this magazine? | | |
| In what ways is this magazine a healthy or unhealthy example of media? | | |

In the space below or on a separate piece of paper, write a paragraph to compare and contrast these two magazines.

# Healthy or Unhealthy?

Do magazines for kids send healthy messages? Or do they send unhealthy messages? Can they send both types of messages to young readers?

**Directions:** Study the magazine cover below and the one on page 100, and then write a paragraph answering the questions for each one.

1. What do you notice about this magazine cover?

2. What obvious messages do you see on this cover?

3. What hidden messages do you see on this cover?

4. In what ways is this cover a healthy or unhealthy example of media?

_____

_____

_____

_____

_____

_____

_____

_____

_____

# Healthy or Unhealthy *(cont.)*

**Directions:** Study the magazine cover below, and then write a paragraph answering the questions.

1. What do you notice about this magazine cover?

2. What obvious messages do you see on this cover?

3. What hidden messages do you see on this cover?

4. In what ways is this cover a healthy or unhealthy example of media?

_____

_____

_____

_____

_____

_____

_____

_____

_____

# Your Favorite Magazine

What is your favorite magazine?  Do you like to read about motorcycles, ice-skating, or horses?

**Directions:**  Choose your favorite magazine.  Study it and answer the questions below.

1. What is the name of this magazine? _____

   _____

2. To what gender, age group, and economic group does this magazine appeal? _____

   _____

3. What are the obvious messages in this magazine? _____

   _____

   _____

   _____

   _____

4. What are the hidden messages in this magazine? _____

   _____

   _____

   _____

   _____

5. In what ways is this magazine a healthy or unhealthy example of media? _____

   _____

   _____

   _____

   _____

   _____

   _____

   _____

   _____

# Design a Healthy Magazine

What types of pictures and words go into a healthy magazine? Make one of your own, and find out! You will need scrap paper and pencils, several sheets of white or colored paper (9" x 11"), markers, stickers, glitter, glue, scissors, three-hole punch, and three metal brads (or ribbon 2' long).

**Directions:**

1. Do you want to make a magazine as a class project? Get into groups of three-to-four students, and then talk about what type of magazine you want to make. Will it be about one topic like food or games? Will it be more general, covering many topics?

2. Talk about what pictures and words will make this a healthy form of media. Write down ideas for your magazine on scrap paper.

3. Decide in your group who is going to write articles and draw pictures or take photos. Decide on a layout for your magazine. Where will the articles go on each page? Where will the illustrations go?

4. Create each page of your magazine. You may want to write and draw on each page. Or, you can write articles and draw pictures on separate pieces of paper. Then you can glue them to the main magazine pages.

5. Use the three-hole punch to carefully punch holes into your magazine pages. Use metal brads to hold the pages together. Or you can weave a ribbon through the holes and tie it in a bow.

6. Finally, pass your magazine around in class for all to enjoy!

# Newspapers

"Extra! Extra! Read All About It!" Newspapers make sure we know what is happening in our world… every day!

This form of media has been around since the 1400s. At that time, newspapers were hand-written. People read them to learn about wars, money, and stories about interesting people.

Sometimes these early newspapers tried to be very exciting. Early German papers reported crimes committed in Transylvania by a count named Vlad Tsepes Drakul . . . otherwise known as Count Dracula!

In 1690, the first newspaper appeared in America. It was called *Publick Occurrences*. It was printed in Boston without approval from the government. The publisher of the newspaper was arrested, and all copies of the newspaper were destroyed.

A hundred years later, people in the American colonies could read many different newspapers. Articles in these papers gave the colonists courage to fight for political independence from England! Thomas Jefferson wrote in 1787, "Were it left to me to decide whether we should have a government without newspapers, or newspapers without a government, I should not hesitate a moment to prefer the latter."

Today, we can read thousands of newspapers in print and on the Internet every day. They are printed in hundreds of languages. Now that's something to shout about!

# Front Pages of the Past

In some ways, newspapers of today are very different from those published hundreds of years ago. In other ways, they are much the same.

**Directions:** Study the front page of the newspaper on page 105. The top left corner states that this was the official newspaper of the A.E.F. Look up the initials "A.E.F." on the Internet. You may want to type "A.E.F. World War I" into your favorite search engine. Next, use the newspaper to complete the crossword puzzle below.

What does A.E.F. stand for? Write it here: _____

**ACROSS**

2. The symbol at the top of the page is a _____.

6. This paper has many stories about _____.

7. This newspaper would appeal mostly to _____.

10. This newspaper was published in the year nineteen hundred and _____.

11. This newspaper cost 50 _____.

**DOWN**

1. At the bottom of the page, there is a _____.

3. A holiday in May is _____.

4. This newspaper was published in the country of _____.

5. The figure in the drawing is a _____.

8. Unlike a newspaper of today, this front page has no _____.

9. This front page implies that soldiers should send their mother a _____.

*The Official Newspaper of the A. E. F.*

# The Stars and Stripes

*By and For the Soldiers of the A. E. F.*

VOL. 2—NO. 13.     FRANCE, FRIDAY, MAY 2, 1919.     PRICE: 50 CENTIMES.

## GREEN DIVISIONS PROVED METTLE IN 2ND ARMY DRIVE

**81st, 7th and 92nd Going Strong When Armistice Intervened**

### PUSH IN DIRECTION OF BRIEY

Operation in Conjunction With French Troops, Would Have Overwhelmed Enemy

## ENGINEERS' WORK SPED DOUGHBOYS TOWARD VICTORY

**Largest of A.E.F.'s Technical Services Had Finger in Every Pie**

### ROSE FROM 6 MEN TO 174,000

Barracks They Built Would, Placed End to End, Stretch 225 Miles, and Railroad Trackage, 947

## "MOTHER'S LETTER"

May 11 is Mother's Day; a week from this Sunday.

## S.O.S. ENDS SOON; THIRD ARMY GIVEN OWN SUPPLY BASE

**May and June to See About 300,000 Leave Back Areas for Home**

### ANTWERP IS KEY TO A. OF O.

Base Sections Will Close, Tours to Grow Smaller as Army Centers More on Rhine

## APRIL DEPARTURES NEARER 300,000 THAN 250,000 SET

**107,083 Sailings in Single Week May Send Month's Total Beyond Schedule**

### S.O.S. GETTING UNDER WAY

Smashing of Records Brings Hope That Half of A.E.F. May Be on Way Home by May 10

## STATE TROOPS MADE PART OF NEW ARMY

**New York, Ohio, New Jersey and Oregon Units Authorized**

## LEAVE MEN MAY GO TO CLOSED AREAS

**B, C, D and E Yanks Can See Resorts Barred to Class A**

## WAY CLEAR TO GIVE TERMS TO GERMANS BEFORE WEEK ENDS

**Italy Cooling Down, While Japan Will Not Press Her Views Now**

## HEATHEN CHINEE IS TRUE TO FORM

*Cleans Up 500 Francs in "Exhibition" Gambling Game*

## FIRST VOLUNTEER RELIEF FOR THIRD ARMY DUE AT BREST

**1,000 Men to Replace Many Now Serving in Occupied Territory**

## BUCK GAINS AGAIN —AS FRANC TUMBLES

**Exchange Rate Going From 5.80 to 6.05 Means Beaucoup on Pay Day**

### THAT LAST SHOT CHANGED

## BOLSHEVIK HENS STRIKE IN COBLENZ

**Why? Their Table of Organization Wasn't Complete**

## SALVATION ARMY DRIVE

Continued on Page 2 — Continued on Page 8

*Image courtesy of the Library of Congress, Serial and Government Publications Division*

# Your Local Paper

Your local newspaper tells so much about your city or town.

**Directions:** Study a copy of your local newspaper and then answer the questions below.

1. What is the name of this newspaper?

2. Who owns this newspaper?

3. How long has this newspaper been published?

4. What is its circulation (that is, how many readers does it have)?

5. What stories appear on the front page?

6. Which story is the most important? How can you tell?

7. Now, examine each section of your local newspaper. In the chart below, name each section. Then, describe it. Explain what types of articles it features. See the example below for details.

| Section | Description | Featured Articles |
|---|---|---|
| Sports | It has stories, calendar events, photos, interviews, and results. | Story on kayaking. Photos of mountain-climbing. Interview with local runner. |
| | | |
| | | |
| | | |
| | | |
| | | |

# The Op/Ed Pages

Look at the Opinion/Editorial pages of your paper to find out what people in your city or town are thinking about.

The editor of the newspaper writes one or two editorials. People just like you write opinion columns and letters to the editor.

**Directions:** Study one Op/Ed page of your local paper. Answer the questions below.

1. What are the editorials about in the Op/Ed pages? _____

   _____

   _____

2. What are the topics of the opinion pieces (not editorials) in the Op/Ed pages? _____

   _____

   _____

3. What topics are mentioned in the letters to the editor in the Op/Ed pages? _____

   _____

   _____

4. Describe what the Op/Ed pages of your local paper say about the people in your town or city. What are their concerns?

   _____

   _____

   _____

   _____

   _____

   _____

   _____

   _____

   _____

   _____

   _____

   _____

   _____

# A Letter to the Editor

You can write a letter to your local newspaper editor. It might even get published! The next two pages will show you how to write a letter and send it to the editor of your newspaper.

**Directions:** Think of an issue that concerns you. Maybe you want to write about the importance of parks in your city. Maybe you want to write in favor of bike helmets. Or maybe you want to write about the importance of picking up litter.

Write a draft of your letter below.

Date: _____

Dear _____ ,

_____

_____

_____

_____

_____

_____

Sincerely,

My Name: _____

Address: _____
Phone: _____
Email: _____

It's easy to send a letter to your local newspaper editor. Some editors prefer letters sent by e-mail. Others like letters sent through the post office. Editors don't always have the space to publish all letters, but they always read them!

**Directions:** Study the *Letters to the Editor* page of your local newspaper for directions on how to send your own letter. Below, write down the steps you must take to submit your letter to the editor.

---

### Steps for Letter Submission

1.

2.

3.

4.

5.

6.

---

Now, look at the letter you wrote on the previous page. Edit it for correct spelling, punctuation, and grammar. Type it on paper or into an e-mail. Ask your teacher or parent to review the letter for appropriate content. Then, send it to the editor. Follow the instructions you wrote above.

Note that you may have more luck getting your letter published if you note your age. Sometimes, an editor will publish a letter the day after it is received. Other times, editors will hold on to your letter for weeks before publishing it.

# Spinning a Story

A spin is an angle from which a reporter can write about a topic. A reporter for the outdoor part of a newspaper wants to write about camping. She could spin the story for parents and write a story about campgrounds that are kid-friendly. Or she could spin the story for people who want to hike 20 miles into the forest.

Different countries may spin one news story in many ways. Why would they do this? One reporter may find a story important to his country. Another might feel the story has little to do with her country. She might write just two paragraphs.

Some reporters might put their opinion into a story. They are not supposed to do this. But sometimes they make a topic seem good or bad. A reporter from Germany may put a good spin on a story about a new road that allows drivers to go 120 miles an hour. But a reporter from the United States might put a bad spin on the same story. This reporter might write that speed causes car wrecks.

**Directions:** Choose one news story from this week. Examine the same story as it is covered in one United States paper, and in newspapers from two other different English speaking countries. You can find foreign newspapers in your public library and on the Internet.

Answer the questions below and on the next page about this story.

1. In one sentence, describe the topic of the news story you have chosen.

2. Write down the names of the three newspapers you used.

3. Study each article for its spin. Can you tell whether each story has a good or bad spin? Explain your answer, below. An example has been given.

| Name of Newspaper | Spin or Angle |
|---|---|
| U.S. Newspaper—*Ontario Examiner* | Puts a bad spin on an article about pet pit bulls. |
| | |
| | |
| | |

# Spinning a Story *(cont.)*

**Directions:** Below, write one paragraph in which you compare the same story as it appears in three different newspapers. Point out how each story is the same.

## Similarities

_____
_____
_____
_____
_____
_____
_____
_____
_____
_____
_____

Now, write one paragraph in which you contrast the same story as it appears in three different newspapers. Point out how each story is different. Pay attention to how each reporter puts a spin on the story.

## Differences

_____
_____
_____
_____
_____
_____
_____
_____
_____
_____
_____

The petroglyphs at Newspaper Rock. Van Gogh's "Sunflowers." The Statue of Liberty. What do these three objects have in common? Each is a work of art. Each is also a form of media.

Humans have always made art. They use their art to talk about the world around them. You can study photographs, paintings, sculptures, and other forms of art just as you would any sort of media.

As an example, look at this photo below. Edward S. Curtis went around the United States and took many photos of Native Americans in the early 1900s. Why did the Native Americans have to move away from their homes in the 1800s and early 1900s? Research this in an encyclopedia, in books, or on the Internet. Write the answer on the lines below.

_____

_____

_____

*Image courtesy of the Library of Congress, Prints and Photographs Division (LC-USZ62-66633)*

**Directions:** Study the image above, and then answer these questions.

| Question | Answer |
| --- | --- |
| Why do you think Edward S. Curtis took so many photos of Native Americans? | |
| What obvious messages exist in this piece of art? | |
| What hidden messages exist in this piece of art? | |
| In what ways is this photo a healthy or unhealthy example of media? | |

# Painting

The history of painting goes back thousands of years. Prehistoric people painted fish and horses on cave walls. Later, painters use their work for political reasons. "Making the Flag," on page 114 shows a group of men gathered around a seamstress.

**Directions:** Study this painting by Jean Louis Jerome Ferris, done in the early 1900s. Then, answer the questions below. Use books, encyclopedias, or the Internet to help you. Once you have answered the questions, follow the directions at the bottom of the page to complete the activity.

1.  What is happening in this painting? You may have to research the seamstress, Betsy Ross, to answer the question. _____

    _____

    _____

2.  When did the action in this painting take place? _____

    _____

    _____

3.  What symbols can you find in this painting? _____

    _____

    _____

4.  What political action was going on in the year when this painting was made? _____

    _____

    _____

5.  Why do you think Ferris chose to paint "Making the Flag" in the early 1900s? What message might he have wanted to send? _____

    _____

    _____

**Directions:** How has the subject matter of painting changed since the early 1900s? How has it stayed the same? Using books, encyclopedias, or the Internet, select a painting made in the last ten years. Sketch it on a separate piece of paper.

Art often gets a brief written description in a museum. Below your sketch, write a description of the painting you chose. Give the artist's name. Explain what is happening in the painting. Note obvious and hidden messages. Share whether you believe this art to be a healthy or unhealthy form of media.

*Image courtesy of the Library of Congress, Prints and Photographs Division (LC-USZ62-823)*

114

# Sculpture

The history of sculpture also goes back to prehistoric times. Most Stone Age artists used ivory or clay for their sculpture. Egyptians used gold and silver for their works of art.

In 1948, two men began to design a sculpture to honor a Lakota leader known as Crazy Horse.

**Directions:** Use books, encyclopedias, and the Internet to study the sculpture above, then fill out the chart.

| | |
|---|---|
| **1.** Who created this sculpture? Where is it located? | |
| **2.** What type of person would enjoy looking at this sculpture? | |
| **3.** Why did this artist choose to sculpt Crazy Horse? | |
| **4.** What obvious message do you find in the way that Crazy Horse is portrayed in this sculpture? | |
| **5.** Do you find any hidden meanings in this sculpture? If so, explain. | |
| **6.** In what ways is this sculpture a healthy or unhealthy form of media? | |

# Sculpture *(cont.)*

Artists have been molding clay and sculpting marble for thousands of years.

Around 1937, an artist named Heinz Warneke sculpted "Tumbling Bears." This sculpture is at the National Zoo in Washington, D.C.

In 1971, sculptor Henry Moore put his piece, "Large Arch" in a front of the public library in Columbus, Indiana.

Both of these sculptures have one thing in common—they represent media!

 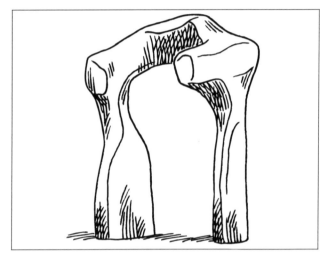

**Directions:** Create your own sculpture as a form of media. You will need a piece of scratch paper, a pencil, a block of clay (any size or color), a small dish of water, and a craft stick for sculpting and defining.

Decide what you will sculpt and sketch a rough draft on your scratch paper. Using your block of clay, create your sculpture. Water will help to mold your clay into a desired shape. Use the craft stick to create sharp details, if needed.

When you have finished, answer these questions.

1. Who is your intended audience for this sculpture? _____

2. What are the obvious messages of your sculpture? _____

_____

_____

3. What are the hidden messages in your sculpture? _____

_____

_____

4. How is this sculpture an example of healthy or unhealthy media? _____

_____

_____

# Photography

Photographs affect people strongly. Photography has been used as a form of media since the late 1800s. It appears on the walls of art galleries. It also appears in newspapers and magazines. Consider the photograph on page 118, which was taken in 1935 by Carl Mydans.

**Directions:** Study the photograph on page 118. Deconstruct it by answering the questions and filling in the chart. Once complete, follow the additional set of directions at the bottom of the page.

| | |
|---|---|
| 1. Using the Internet, books, or encyclopedias, explain The Great Depression. Also note when it took place. | |
| 2. What do you think is happening in this photo? | |
| 3. What obvious messages exist in this photograph? | |
| 4. What hidden messages exist in this photograph? | |
| 5. How does this photograph make you feel? | |
| 6. How is this photograph a healthy or unhealthy example of media? | |

**Directions:** How is photography used as media today? What messages does it send to people who see it? Choose a photo from a magazine or newspaper. Paste or sketch it on a separate piece of paper.

Now, describe this photograph in one paragraph. Who would like this photo? What obvious messages do you see? What hidden messages can you find? How does this photo make you feel? Is this photo a healthy or unhealthy example of media?

Image courtesy of the Library of Congress, Prints and Photographs Division (LC-USZ62-130013)

# Comics

Comic strips first started to appear in newspapers in the early 1900s. One of the first comics was called "The Yellow Kid." The Yellow Kid was a bald child in a yellow nightshirt. He liked to hang around in the alley. People could read The Yellow Kid comic strip in the Sunday paper.

Charles Schultz started his daily Peanuts comic strip in the 1950s. Kids and adults loved to read about Snoopy, Charlie Brown, Lucy, and the rest of the gang. You can still read the Peanuts comic strip in newspapers today.

In 1900, an artist named Frederick Opper began to draw his comic strip called "Happy Hooligan." His main character was a kind but gullible man named "Happy."

The comic book was invented in the 1930s. Superman was one of the first heroes in comics. Batman and Robin, Wonder Woman, the Green Hornet, Captain America, and other superheroes appeared in the pages of comic books as well.

**Directions:** Study the frame of a Happy Hooligan comic strip on page 120. Answer the questions below.

| | |
|---|---|
| 1. Who are the main characters in this comic frame? | |
| 2. What do Happy Hooligan's clothes say about his character? | |
| 3. What do the police officer's clothes say about his character? | |
| 4. How would you describe the expression on the dog's face? | |
| 5. What details make the police officer appear more powerful than Happy Hooligan? | |
| 6. What do you think happened to cause Happy Hooligan to get arrested? | |

**Directions:** Study the Happy Hooligan comic frame. Then, draw what you think happened before his arrest in the blank frames below.

The first Japanese comic books were called *manga*. They appeared in the 18th century. Manga means "unusual pictures."

Today, many manga have black and white drawings and just a few color pages. They inspire anime. This is animation that becomes part of a television show or movie.

**Directions:** Find two comic books. One should be from the United States and one should be from Japan. Study them and then compare and contrast these comics in the space below.

1. What is the plot of each of these comic books? Describe it in a few sentences.

   a. _____

   b. _____

2. Describe the art in each comic book. Is it in color or black and white? How are people and animals shown? Are the drawings simple or complicated?

   a. _____

   _____

   b. _____

   _____

3. What do you see as the same about these two comic books?

   a. _____

   _____

   b. _____

   _____

4. How are these two comic books different? Write a couple of sentences to explain.

   _____

   _____

   _____

   _____

5. Are these comic books examples of healthy or unhealthy media? Explain your answer.

   _____

   _____

   _____

   _____

# Graffiti and Murals

What do you think when you see a bad word spray-painted on the side of a building? What do you think when you see a complex and colorful mural outside a store?

Graffiti and murals are both forms of media. Study the different definitions below.

| |
|---|
| **Graffiti**—Initials, slogans, or drawings on a wall or sidewalk. |
| **Mural**—A large picture on a wall or ceiling. |

**Directions:** Study the images below and then, on a separate piece of paper, write out sentences 1–4 for each image, filling in the blanks to complete.

**Image One**

**Image Two**

1. This is a picture of _____.

2. The lifestyle presented in this image is _____.

3. The technique of persuasion used in this image is _____.

4. Is this a healthy or unhealthy form of media? _____.

Finally, write a paragraph to answer the question below.

Why do you think that murals often get positive attention, while graffiti often gets negative attention? Explain your answer.

_____

_____

_____

_____

_____

_____

# Create a Mural

You can create a mural to brighten your classroom! You will need scratch paper, butcher paper (enough to cover one classroom bulletin board), tape or staples, pencils with erasers, paintbrushes (both thick and thin, one for each person), cans of water-based paint in many colors, newspaper, clean-up rags, and water.

**Directions:**

1. Cover a bulletin board with butcher paper. Tape or staple the paper to the back of the board.

2. Decide as a group what your mural will look like. You might want to make it as a class or break into groups of four and sketch a small section of the mural on your own. Draw your designs with a pencil on scratch paper.

3. Get ready to paint! Gather rags and water for cleaning up. Spread newspaper below the wall so you don't get paint on the floor. Outline your mural idea with small brushes and paint. Then, fill in the outlines with paint.

4. Allow the paint to dry. Wash brushes well.

5. Finally, answer the questions below.

| | |
|---|---|
| **1.** What age group and gender would like your mural? | |
| **2.** What obvious messages are in your mural? | |
| **3.** What hidden messages are in your mural? | |
| **4.** What methods of advertising do you use in your mural? | |
| **5.** In what ways is your mural a healthy or unhealthy example of media? | |

# Websites

Websites appear as soon as you log onto the Internet. Words, pictures, and ads make websites a complicated form of media.

Who is trying to sell you a product or idea on the Internet? What are the effects of ads on your feelings and actions? When you can answer these questions, you will be a media literate consumer of websites.

**Directions:** Study the sample website above, then answer these questions.

1. What gender and age group would like this website? _____

_____

2. How many news stories can you count on this website? _____

_____

3. How many ads can you count on this website? _____

_____

4. Why do you think this photo was chosen for this website? _____

_____

_____

5. In what ways is this website a healthy or unhealthy example of media? _____

_____

_____

# Popular Home Pages

A home page is the main page of a website. It gives a big "hello" to visitors. It offers photos and gives links to click for more web pages. There are thousands of home pages on the Internet. You can find them for cooking, for pets, and for racecars. They exist for tennis and dolls and travel. Do you have a favorite home page?

**Directions:** Choose one home page to study. Not sure which one to choose? Type the keywords *home page* into a search engine along with a word to describe your favorite subject. With adult supervision, click on one of the links that comes up. Study the home page. Then, fill in the blanks to create a short report, below.

I am here today to talk about the home page called _____.

It's a very _____ homepage that will appeal to _____

who are _____ years old.

The creator of this page used a few methods of advertising. These include _____,

_____, and _____. I can see that the obvious messages on

this home page tell viewers to _____. But look carefully! You will also find

hidden messages that tell visitors to _____ and _____.

Study this home page for yourself. I think you will find it a (n) _____ form

of media.

# Websites for Children

The Internet hosts hundreds of websites for kids. Do you like science? There are websites for kids who are interested in any type of science, from biology to chemistry. Do you love dogs? There are websites to teach you to care for your pet, and to train it. There are even websites with photos of dogs that are available for adoption.

**Directions:** Search for a kids' website based on the list below. In your search engine, type *kids* and the name of the topic that interests you. Then, answer the questions.

- history
- nature
- math
- music

- animals
- science
- sports
- movies

- games
- art
- books
- celebrities

| | |
|---|---|
| **1.** What is the name of this home page? | |
| **2.** What gender and age group will like this home page? | |
| **3.** What methods of advertising do you see on this home page? | |
| **4.** What are the obvious messages on this home page? | |
| **5.** What are the hidden messages on this home page? | |
| **6.** How is this home page an example of healthy or unhealthy media? | |

# Author Websites

Who is your favorite author? Many authors have a website. On it, they post photos and interviews, information on their books, and calendars to let readers know when they will be giving readings from their books.

**Directions:** Choose your favorite author. Locate his or her website with the help of your favorite search engine. The keywords should include the author's name and the words *home page*. Below, write a letter to your author. Discuss his or her website. What parts of the website do you like? Which do you feel could be better? Comment on obvious and hidden messages on the website. Also tell the author whether you feel the website is a healthy or unhealthy form of media.

Date: _____

Dear _____ ,

_____

_____

_____

_____

_____

_____

_____

_____

Sincerely,

_____

# Podcasts

A podcast is news and/or entertainment that you can find on the Internet. You can download it on your computer and listen to it on your headphones.

There are many podcasts made for kids. One of the most popular types is a music podcast. This kind of podcast will include songs and interviews with musicians.

**Directions:** Download and listen to a podcast about kids' music. In your favorite search engine, type in the key words *children's music podcast*. Listen to it carefully. Then, write a two-minute review of this music podcast. In it, note the following things.

- the name of the podcast
- the host's name
- special guests
- sponsors who helped to pay for this podcast

- who would enjoy this podcast
- methods of advertising used in this podcast
- obvious and hidden messages in the podcast
- whether this podcast is healthy or unhealthy

_____

_____

_____

_____

_____

_____

_____

_____

_____

_____

_____

_____

_____

Read your written podcast aloud once to rehearse. Then read it and record it on your computer as a sound file. Need information on how to make a podcast? Type the words *record a podcast* into your favorite search engine.

Once your podcast is formatted as a sound file on your computer, you can play it for everyone to hear.

# Build a Website

Learn about how people make websites by building your own! You will need scratch paper, pencils with erasers, and a computer.

**Directions**

1. First you need to think about how many pages you want your website to be. Include a home page, and at least one other page. On scratch paper, sketch a design for your website pages. Decide whether you will include ads and photos. You may want to ask different people in your group to make different web pages.

2. Write the words and sketch pictures for your website, on scratch paper.

3. You may choose to build this website on a computer. There are many sites that let you build a site for free. They use a template that is easy to follow. To find a site, type the key words *free website building for kids* into your favorite search engine.

4. Follow the computer instructions to build your website. Type in words and upload your photos. You may want to scan your artwork and upload it, too. Note that it is illegal to upload someone else's writing and pictures from the Internet.

5. Ask your teacher to review your website. After he or she has given you permission, give your friends and family the link to your website so that they may see it, too!

6. Finally, fill in the blanks below to describe your website.

My website will appeal to people who are _____ and _____.

I used the following methods of advertising: _____,

_____ , and _____.

There are a few obvious messages on my web site. They are _____ and

_____ . I have also included a few hidden messages.

They are _____ and _____. I hope that you will find my

website an _____ form of media.

# Final Project

Congratulations! You are almost finished with your study of Media Literacy. Now, show your understanding of this subject. It's time to make a final project and analyze it!

**Directions:** Choose a final project to make from the box below. Then, analyze it in a short essay. Make sure to use all of the terms you have learned to describe your media creation. Include the following details:

- your audience
- obvious messages
- methods of advertising
- hidden messages
- healthy or unhealthy media

---

## Forms of Media

- billboard
- comic book
- magazine
- newspaper
- package
- painting
- photograph
- podcast
- print ad
- radio ad
- recorded song
- sculpture
- television commercial
- website

---

_____

_____

_____

_____

_____

_____

_____

_____

_____

_____

_____

_____

_____

_____

# Certificate

This is to certify that
_____

has become a media-literate consumer,
skilled in the analysis of:

- Advertisements
- Art
- Magazines
- Movies
- Music
- Newspapers

- Packaging
- Product Placement
- Radio
- Television
- Video Games
- Websites

Signed this _____ of _____.

_____
Teacher's Signature

# Answer Key

**Page 10 —** How Much Media?

1. Students list forms of media they see and hear daily.

2. Students chart how many hours a day they see and hear various forms of media.

3. Students record observations on their media use.

**Page 11 —** Media's Importance to You

1. Students write down a favorite form of media and how it affects them.

**Page 14 —** Advertising in Action

Students write down one slogan and one jingle.

**Page 15 —** Hidden Messages

1. Obvious—drink this chocolate milk.

   Hidden—if you drink this chocolate milk, you will be popular and able to dance well.

2. Obvious—do your homework.

   Hidden—if you do your homework, you will be rich and successful.

3. Obvious—wear your bicycle helmet.

   Hidden—if you don't wear your bicycle helmet, you could die.

**Page 16 —** Propaganda

1. b

2. c

3. a

**Page 18 —** Making Propaganda

Grade students for effort and understanding of how one ad constitutes propaganda.

**Page 19—**Stereotypes

1. Completed as example.

2. Both the woman and man are being stereotyped. She is shown as the primary shopper, and he is shown as not participating in grocery shopping. Both men and women might be hurt by this media because it suggests rigid gender roles.

3. Both bears are stereotyped. In this book, the blond character is viewed as desirable, while the red-haired bear is not. Children might be hurt by this media that disparages red hair and old clothes.

4. Teachers are stereotyped as "fools" and "jerks." They may be hurt by this media which makes fun of them. Students may be hurt as well if they grow up disrespecting teachers to the point where they refuse to learn.

**Page 20 —** Stereotypes (*cont.*)

Grade students on effort and understanding of stereotypes.

**Page 21** — Healthy and Unhealthy Media
Ad One

1. True
2. False
3. False
4. True
5. True

Ad Two

1. False
2. True
3. True
4. True
5. False

**Page 24** — First Media
Grade students for effort and thoughtfulness.

**Page 25** — Understanding Petroglyphs
Grade students for effort and accuracy.

**Page 26** — Make a Petroglyph
Grade students for effort and thoughtfulness.

**Page 27** — Print Ads

1. horse invigorator
2. Rosenberg
3. adult men
4. hyperbole, beautiful people
5. Give this invigorator to your horse.
6. You will be a strong, handsome, powerful man if you use this product.
7. Open to student interpretation. Some students may worry about the horse's obvious discomfort in this ad.

**Page 29** — Early Print Ads
Ad One

1. flavoring extracts

2. A.W. Harrison

3. adult women and men

4. plain folks, beautiful people

5. Buy these extracts because they are the best in the world.

6. If you use these extracts, you will be popular and attractive.

7. Healthy, unless the extracts are toxic.

Ad Two

1. American Cream Soap

2. American Soap Company

3. adult women

4. hyperbole, beautiful people, humor

5. Buy this soap.

6. If you buy this soap, you will be calm, happy, and industrious.

7. Open to interpretation. Students may point out that the gender stereotypes are unhealthy. They may point out that soap is a healthy product.

**Page 32** — Today's Print Ads
Grade for effort and understanding of print ads.

**Page 33** — Compare and Contrast
Grade for effort and understanding of how print ads have changed over time.

**Page 35** — Make a Print Ad
Grade for effort and understanding of student's own print ad as media.

**Page 37** — Early Billboards
Billboard One

1. Women in Colorado should vote against Woodrow Wilson and the Democratic candidate for Congress.

2. The National Woman's Party

3. women of voting age

4. Make sure all women in the nation can vote by voting against Wilson.

5. Women in Colorado have an obligation to women around the nation.

6. Open to student interpretation. Most will feel that women's suffrage was a good thing.

**Page 38 —** Early Billboards (*cont.*)
Billboard Two

1. b
2. d
3. c
4. a
5. e

**Page 39 —** Billboards of Today
Grade for effort and depth of analysis.

**Pages 41–42 —** Compare and Contrast
Grade for effort and understanding of how billboards have changed over time.

**Page 43 —** Make a Billboard
Grade for effort and understanding of own billboard as a form of media.

**Page 45 —** Radio Ads

1. Completed as example
2. beautiful people—use actors with sultry, elegant voices
3. fear—use suspenseful music, screaming, windows breaking
4. warm and fuzzy— kittens mewing, puppies yapping, cute children's voices, lullabies and nursery rhymes, lambs or other baby animals calling
5. symbols—patriotic music, recognizable tunes like Richard Wagner's "Bridal Chorus," alarm clocks, roosters crowing to symbolize morning, crickets to symbolize night, etc.
6. humor—particularly high- or low-pitched voices, yodeling, tongue-twisters, funny squeaks or slide-whistles, goats bleating, etc.
7. testimonials—use people with "everyday" voices to talk about a product's worth enthusiastically
8. repetition—repeat a song, a brand name, or a slogan
9. scientific evidence—use a British actor to present evidence in a formal, elegant tone. Have machinery sounds in the background.

**Page 46 —** Historic Radio Ads
Grade for effort and student understanding of radio ads from the past.

**Pages 47 —** Today's Radio Ads
Grade for effort and student understanding of radio ads from the present time.

**Page 48 —** Record a Radio Ad
Grade for effort and student understanding of own radio ad as a form of media.

**Pages 49–50 —** The First Radio Shows
Grade for student understanding of radio shows from the past.

**Page 51 — War of the Worlds**

1. A narrator introduces the story, and then a radio newscast begins. Music plays, and is abruptly interrupted by the announcer saying that Martians have landed on Earth.

2. People who didn't catch the introduction to this radio piece, and who tuned in only to the simulated broadcast with its reports of Martians landing and scientists confirming this, truly believed Martians had landed on Earth.

3. This is open to students' interpretation. Look for reasonable, thoughtful answers.

**Page 52 — Radio Shows and Podcasts**
Grade for effort and depth of student analysis.

**Page 53 — Record a Radio Show**
Grade for effort and student understanding of own radio show as a form of media.

**Page 55 — Your Television Journal**
Grade for student effort and level of detail.

**Page 57 — Classic Television Ads**
Grade for effort and depth of analysis.

**Page 58 — Today's Television Ads**
Grade for effort and depth of analysis.

**Page 59 — Compare and Contrast**
Grade for effort and depth of student understanding of how television ads have changed over time.

**Page 60 — Create a Television Ad**
Grade for effort and student understanding of own television ad as a form of media.

**Page 61 — Television News**
Grade for effort and level of detail.

**Page 62 — Healthy Television News?**
Grade for effort and understanding of the effects of television news segments.

**Page 63 — The Role of Sponsors**
Grade for effort and understanding of sponsors and their connection to television programs.

**Page 64 — Hidden Messages in TV**
Grade for effort and understanding of obvious and hidden messages on television.

**Page 65 — Turn Off Your Television**
Grade for effort and depth of analysis.

**Page 66 — No TV? What to Do?**
Grade for effort and creativity in thinking of alternatives to watching television.

**Page 67 — TV–Turnoff Week Journal**
Grade for effort and depth of description.

**Page 68 — Music**
Grade for effort and depth of thought.

**Page 69** — Conflicts in Music

1. A listener would benefit from file sharing by getting free music and having an online community with which to chat about music. However, someone downloading music for free might have to pay a hefty penalty, and might even go to jail.

2. A musician would benefit from people file sharing music because of increased exposure and publicity. The musician would be harmed by decreased music sales.

Grade student compositions for effort and understanding of one controversial issue as it relates to music.

**Page 70** — Analyze a Song

Grade for effort and depth of analysis.

**Page 71** — Music Videos

1. Girls and young women would likely enjoy this video.

2. warm and fuzzy, bandwagon, beautiful people

3. One lifestyle is a student lifestyle. The other is a more glamorous rock-and-roll lifestyle.

4. The obvious message in this video is that if someone feels lost and lonely, he or she should come and sit at the narrator's table and share a laugh.

5. The hidden message in this video is open to student interpretation. Students may say that the hidden message is about the importance of befriending new kids at school.

6. Open to student interpretation.

**Page 72** — Music Videos (*cont.*)

Grade for effort and analysis of chosen video.

**Page 73** — Make a Music Video

Grade for effort and understanding of how to write and create a music video.

**Page 74** — Videogames

1. Grade for effort and ability to recognize differences in videogame consoles.

2.–4. Grade for effort and depth of analysis.

**Page 75** — Videogame Ads

1. In The Doghouse

2. FunGamz

3. "Who Let the Dogs In?"

4. Obvious message—Help Pooch to Find his Way from Your Bed to His Doghouse.

5. Hidden message—Dogs should not sleep in people's beds.

6. open to student interpretation

**Page 76** — Videogame Ads (*cont.*)

Grade for effort and understanding of how to deconstruct a videogame print advertisement.

**Page 77** — Violence in Videogames

Grade for effort and understanding of a favorite videogame, as well as how violence may appear in this game.

**Page 78** — Your Body and Feelings

Grade for effort and depth of thought regarding physical and emotional effects of playing videogames.

# Answer Key *(cont.)*

**Page 79 —** Your Favorite Videogame

Grade for effort and depth of thought regarding student's favorite videogame.

**Page 80 —** Videogame Debate

Grade each student team for effort, as well as for depth of thought in formulating and presenting arguments.

**Page 82 —** Packages of the Past

Unrivaled = has no competitor in terms of quality.

1. D. Spaulding & Co.

2. people who need glue for projects

3. This buckskin glue is unrivaled.

4. If you use this glue, your family will bond together happily.

5. plain folks, warm and fuzzy, hyperbole—all are correct

**Page 83 —** Packages of Today

Grade for effort and understanding of how to deconstruct a contemporary package label.

**Page 84 —** Color, Shape, and Words

1. blue

2. an usual shape such as a hexagon or a pyramid

3. green

4. purple

5. a superhero or cartoon character

6. red, yellow, or orange

7. information on dosage, contents, how it helps consumers, side-effects, testimonials, ounces

**Pages 85 —** Compare and Contrast

Grade for effort and student understanding of how packages have changed over time.

**Page 87 —** Design a Package

Grade for effort and understanding of how to design and make an effective package label.

**Page 89 —** Product Placement in Action

Grade for effort and understanding of product placement in movie trailers.

**Page 90 —** Products in Books

1. Cookies are used as alphabet practice.

2. Students will likely note that the cookie manufacturer paid for the product to appear in the book. However, some may consider whether the publisher paid for the privilege of featuring this cookie.

3. Children who are just learning their letters will enjoy this book—ages 2–5.

4. Readers will learn their alphabet.

5. Readers may learn to love and desire cookies. They may learn to see sugar as linked with reading.

6. Some students may say that this media is healthy because it's educational and fun. Others may say that this media is unhealthy because it teaches children to love a brand-name fattening product in the guise of an alphabet book.

**Page 91** — Products in Videogames

1. Advertisers want to put their products in videogames so that players will see and desire these products.

2. Videogame designers agree to feature name-brand products in their games because they are paid, and/or because it gives the games a more realistic quality.

3. Students will have varying views. Some may like product placement in videogames because they enjoy the product or agree that it gives a game a more realistic quality. Others may feel that advertisers are force-feeding them messages to buy a brand-name product.

4. Students' answers will vary. Some may say that people play videogames without even noticing product placement. Others will note that subconsciously, players see and desire these products. Students may note that players deliberately buy products featured in videogames, believing the items to be part of a desirable lifestyle.

Grade for effort and understanding of how to place a product into a videogame.

**Page 92** — Products on Television

Grade for effort and understanding of how to locate product placement in a television show.

**Page 93** — Taste-Test!

Grade for effort and depth of thought.

**Page 94** — Products in Movies

Grade for effort and student attempts to locate product placement in a movie.

**Page 95**—Magazines

1. Vanity Fair

2. women from 12 and up

3. Three well-dressed women gather with one little boy and a dog. The title implies that they may be vain about their appearance.

4. The hidden message is that if you buy this magazine, you too will be glamorous and popular.

**Page 97** — Tricks in Photography *(cont.)*

Open to student interpretation. Students may guess any or all of the outcomes given for each scene.

**Page 98** — Magazines for Children

Grade for effort and depth of analysis regarding magazines and how they compare and contrast to one another.

**Page 99** — Healthy or Unhealthy?

1. Students may note that the beautiful kids stand out on this cover, along with flashy graphics and fonts.

2. The obvious message on this cover is that being attractive is important for happiness and success.

3. Students may see hidden messages including one that says thin is beautiful, that only thin and beautiful people find boy/girlfriends, that sex appeal is critical, and looks are of vast importance.

4. Students may point out that this media is healthy because it teaches you how to dress in the latest fashions and be popular. More likely, they'll point out that the focus on image and clothing is shallow and can contribute to insecurity and eating disorders.

**Page 100—Healthy or Unhealthy?** *(cont.)*

1. Students may point out the intrigue of kids helping a baby bird, along with the affirmative title and interesting headlines. They may note that the kids on the cover don't look like supermodels.

2. The obvious message is that life is interesting, and full of fun and helpful things to do.

3. Students may find hidden messages telling them that service to others is important, that spending time in nature is desirable, and that students have a responsibility to help the earth.

4. Most will likely say that this is a healthy form of media because of its suggestions for wholesome activities.

**Page 101 —** Your Favorite Magazine

Grade for effort and depth of analysis of student's favorite magazine.

**Page 102 —** Design a Healthy Magazine

Grade for effort and student understanding of what constitutes a healthy magazine.

**Page 104 —** Front Pages of the Past

A.E.F. stands for American Expeditionary Force

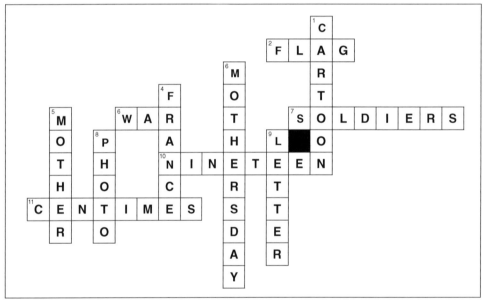

**Page 106 —** Your Local Paper

Grade for effort and student analysis of a local paper.

**Page 107 —** The Op/Ed Section

Grade for effort and understanding of the op-ed section of student's local paper.

**Page 108 —** A Letter to the Editor

Grade for effort, readability, and clarity of opinion.

**Page 110 —** Spinning a Story

Grade for effort and understanding of spins and how they are used in three stories covering the same topic.

**Page 111 —** Spinning a Story *(cont.)*

Grade for effort and depth of thought in comparing and contrasting three newspaper articles.

**Page 112** — Art

1. The United States Government forcibly removed the Native Americans from much of their land and made them live on reservations.

2. Open to student interpretation. He wanted to document their way of life and their plight.

3. These men are civilized and hard working.

4. Open to student interpretation. Students may see them as resentful or distrustful of the camera and the white photographer.

5. Open to student interpretation. Students will likely say that this is a healthy form of media because the government gets a chance to consider Native Americans as people and will possibly treat them with more respect.

**Page 113** — Painting

1. In this painting, Betsy Ross sews the first official flag of the U.S. while George Washington, Robert Morris, and George Ross look on.

2. 1776

3. The flag is the most prominent symbol of the U.S.

4. The Revolutionary War was taking place.

5. Open to student interpretation. The artist may have responded to WWI with this painting to remind the U.S. of the importance of freedom from government oppression.

6. Students' sketches—Grade for effort and depth of thought in student analysis of art.

**Page 115** — Sculpture

1. Sculptor Korczak Ziolkowski and Lakota Chief Henry sculpted this piece. It is located in the Black Hills of South Dakota.

2. Someone interested in American History and/or art would like this sculpture.

3. These artists wanted to sculpt Crazy Horse as both a memorial to the Lakota leader, and as a tribute to Native Americans.

4. The obvious message is that the subject of this art is brave and powerful.

5. The hidden message might be that the U.S. government should not have displaced the Native Americans. Students might say that the hidden message is one of Native American resilience.

6. Open to student interpretation.

**Page 116** — Sculpture *(cont.)*

Grade for effort and understanding of sculpture as a form of media.

**Page 117 —** Photography

1. The Great Depression took place in the 1930s. Thousands of families lost their jobs and their homes. The Dust Bowl claimed farmland—people were unable to grow food and headed west to look for migrant positions picking crops.

2. In this photo, children play and talk in rubble.

3. The obvious message in this photo is that these children are poor. They have to play among trash in the dirt.

4. Hidden messages are open to interpretation. Students might point out that the hidden message is that the government must give these children economic aid.

5. Open to student interpretation.

6. Students will likely say that this is a healthy form of media as it raises public awareness of the plight of children during the Great Depression. Others may say that it is unhealthy propaganda that breeds fear and panic.

Photo—Grade for effort and student understanding of photography as media.

**Page 119 —** Comics

1. The main characters are Happy Hooligan, a police officer, and a dog.

2. Students will likely say that Happy's ragged clothes and tiny hat show that he doesn't care how he looks. They may observe that he appears to be carefree.

3. Students may observe that the officer's suit and hat show him to be rigid and professional.

4. Open to student interpretation.

5. The police officer appears more powerful because he is brandishing a nightstick, and he has Happy by the shirt collar. He's also a taller, larger man.

6. Open to student interpretation.

**Page 121 —** Comics *(cont.)*

Grade for effort and depth of thought in comparing and contrasting comic books from the U.S. and Japan.

**Page 122—**Graffiti and Murals

**Image One**

1. graffiti
2. mean/tough/urban
3. bandwagon
4. unhealthy

**Image Two**

1. a retired teacher
2. sweet
3. warm and fuzzy
4. healthy

Grade paragraph for effort and understanding on murals and graffiti

**Page 123** — Create a Mural
Grade for effort and understanding of what constitutes a healthy mural.

**Page 124** — Websites

1. Sixth-graders of both genders will enjoy this website.

2. At least three news stories appear.

3. At least seven ads appear.

4. Students may observe that this photo was chosen because the boy is attractive and fit, which draws viewers to the site.

5. Students may say that this web page is healthy because it offers news—especially a reminder to pick up litter. They may find that it is unhealthy because it has so many advertisements, and a focus on the idea that thin and attractive is most desirable.

**Page 125** — Popular Home Pages
Grade for effort and depth of analysis of one home page.

**Page 126** — Websites for Children
Grade for effort and depth of analysis of one website and how it appeals to young people.

**Page 127** — Author Websites
Grade for effort and depth of analysis of one author's home page and healthy/unhealthy messages.

**Page 128** — Podcasts
Grade for effort and understanding of both how to create, and how to analyze, a podcast.

**Page 129** — Build a Website
Grade for effort and understanding of how to create and build a website as a form of media.

**Page 130** — Final Project
Grade final project for effort, and for demonstration of components of media literacy as covered in this book.

# Resources

## For Further Study

### Books

Andersen, Neil. *At the Controls: Questioning Video and Computer Games.* Fact Finders, 2007.

Baker, Frank W. *Coming Distractions: Questioning Movies.* Capstone Press, 2007

Baran, Stanley J. *Introduction to Mass Communication: Media Literacy and Culture.* McGraw-Hill, 2003.

Botzakis, Stergios. *Pretty in Pink: Questioning Magazines.* Fact Finders, 2007.

Silverblatt, Art. *Media Literacy: Keys to Interpreting Media Messages.* Praeger, 2001.

Wan, Guofang. *TV Takeover: Questioning Television.* Fact Finders, 2007.

| Organizations | |
|---|---|
| Center for Media Literacy | http://www.medialit.org/ |
| Media Education Foundation | http://www.mediaed.org/ |
| New Mexico Media Literacy Project | http://www.nmmlp.org/ |
| Northwest Media Literacy Center | http://www.mediathink.org/ |
| **Websites** | |
| General portal for media literacy education | http://www1.medialiteracy.com/ |
| Media literacy clearinghouse | http://www.frankwbaker.com/ |
| Tools for teaching media literacy | http://www.mediachannel.org/classroom/ |
| Media activism site | http://www.mediawatch.com/ |

Manufactured by Amazon.ca
Bolton, ON

15212781R00081